"This book is God's warning to this generation—if you have ever doubted the existence of hell, DON'T!"
—*Marilyn Hickey, Denver, Colorado*

"I have read this book, trembling in my heart. I do believe that Rev. Baxter had a true encounter with the reality of hell in her experience of revelation by Jesus Christ our Lord." —*David Yonggi Cho, Seoul, Korea*

"Mary Baxter truly has an incredible testimony that needs to be shared with all. God surely is using Mary as a soul winner for Jesus Christ."
—*Eldred Thomas, President, KLTJ–TV,*
Houston, Texas

"This is one of the most powerful testimonies I have ever read! Mary's descriptions of hell are so real that readers will feel that they are right there with her as Jesus is showing her the horrors of the pit. I wish this book could be made available to everyone—to Christians as a warning to continue walking with Jesus, and to non-Christians to show them what is awaiting them if they do not commit their lives to Jesus Christ."
—*R. Russell Bixler, Chairman/CEO,*
Cornerstone TV, Wall, Pennsylvania

"Unlike many other books, I believe that the Holy Spirit has brought this writing into being for time and eternity. The experiences and the message are of utmost importance to the body of Christ. I believe that God's anointing will rest upon this book and minister to every person who reads these contents."
—*T. L. Lowery, Pastor, Washington, D. C.*

A DIVINE
REVELATION
OF
HELL

A
DIVINE
REVELATION
OF

HELL

MARY K. BAXTER

Whitaker House

A DIVINE REVELATION OF HELL

ISBN: 0-88368-279-6
Printed in the United States of America
Copyright © 1993 by Dr. T. L. Lowery

Whitaker House
30 Hunt Valley Circle
New Kensington, PA 15068

For speaking engagements
by Mary K. Baxter contact:
Dr. T. L. Lowery
National Church of God
6700 Bock Road
Fort Washington, MD 20744

Library of Congress Cataloging-in-Publication Data

Baxter, Mary K.
    A divine revelation of hell / Mary K. Baxter.
        p.   cm.
    ISBN 0-88368-279-6 (trade paper)
    1. Hell—Christianity. 2. Private revelations. 3. Visions.
4. Baxter, Mary K.   I. Title
BT838.B35   1997
236'.25—dc21   96-49171

11 12 13 14 15 16 17 / 07 06 05 04 03 02 01

Contents

Foreword

Marcus Bach stated that books are often referred to as brain children, and rightly so. Not unlike the children of one's flesh and blood, these creative siblings, born by choice or chance are destined to have lives of their own. Their experiences in the world compare favorably to those of any other seminal offering. All of the human emotions are theirs. And no doubt their secret fear is that they may someday be permanently shelved and forgotten.

Unlike other books, I believe that the Holy Spirit has brought this writing into being for time and eternity. The experiences and the message are of utmost importance to the body of Christ. I believe that God's anointing will rest upon this book and minister to every person who reads these contents.

Dedication

This work is dedicated to the glory of
God the Father,
God the Son and
God the Holy Spirit,
Without Whom this book would not be possible.

Introduction

I recognize that without the supernatural power of the Lord Jesus Christ, this book nor any other which proposes to deal with the afterlife could be written. Jesus alone holds the keys to hell and has paid the price for our entrance to heaven.

I found that writing this book was a long, lonely, demanding experience. In fact, the book has waited several years to be revealed. The revelations from the Lord came to me in 1976. It took eight months to put it on paper. The writing of the manuscript itself covered a period of several years and putting the Scripture references in step-by-step order took another year. Finalizing the book took the best part of the winter of 1982 and the year 1983. In addition, for a period of thirty nights, Jesus took me into hell, followed by ten nights of visits to heaven.

I see now that the Lord was preparing me to write this book when even as a child I had dream about God. After I was born again, I had a very strong love for the lost and wanted to see souls saved.

After the Lord appeared to me in 1976 and told me that I was chosen for a special assignment, He said, "My child, I will manifest myself to you to bring people out of darkness into light. For the Lord God has chosen you for a purpose: to write and make a record of the things I will show and tell you.

"I am going to reveal unto you the reality of hell, that many may be saved, many will repent of their evil ways before it is too late.

"Your soul will be taken out of your body, by me, the Lord Jesus Christ, and transmitted into hell and other places that I want you to see. I will also show you visions of heaven and other places and give you many revelations."

Mary Kathryn Baxter

To Kathryn from Jesus

For this purpose you were born, to write and tell what I have shown and told you. For these things are faithful and true. Your call is to let the world know there is a hell and that I, Jesus, was sent by God to save them from this torment.

1

Into Hell

In March 1976 while I was praying at home, I had a visit from the Lord Jesus Christ. I had been praying in the Spirit for days when all at once I felt the very presence of God. His power and His glory filled the house. A brilliant light illuminated the room where I was praying, and a sweet and wonderful feeling came over me.

Lights flowed in billows, rolling and folding into one another and rolling over and out of each other. It was a spectacular sight! And then the voice of the Lord began to speak to me.

He said, "I am Jesus Christ, your Lord, and I wish to give you a revelation to prepare the saints for My return and to turn many to righteousness. The powers of darkness are real and My judgments are true.

"My child, I will take you into hell by My Spirit, and I will show you many things which I want the world to know. I will appear to you many times; I will take your spirit out of your body and will actually take you into hell.

"I want you to write a book and tell of the visions and of all the things I reveal to you. You and I will walk through hell together. Make a record of these things which were and are and are to come. My words are true, faithful and trustworthy. I Am That I Am, and there is none beside Me."

"Dear Lord," I cried out, "What do You want me to do?" My whole being wanted to cry out to Jesus, to acknowledge His presence. The best I can describe it is to say love came over me. It was the most beautiful, peaceful, joyful, powerful love I have ever felt.

God's praises began to flow from me. All at once I wanted to give Him my whole life to be used by Him, to help save people from their sin. I knew, by His Spirit, that it actually was Jesus the Son of God who was there in the room with me. I cannot find words to express His divine presence. But I know that I know it was the Lord.

"Behold, My child," Jesus said, "I am going to take you by My Spirit into hell so that you may be able to make a record of the reality of it, to tell the whole earth that hell is real, and to bring the lost out of darkness and into the light of the gospel of Jesus Christ."

Instantly, my soul was taken out of my body. I went with Jesus up out of my room and into the sky. I knew all that was going on about me. I saw my husband and children asleep in our home below.

It was as though I had died and my body was left behind on the bed while my spirit was going with Jesus up through the top of the house. It seemed as though the whole roof was rolled back, and I could see my family asleep in their beds.

I felt the touch of Jesus as He said, "Fear not. They will be safe." He knew my thoughts.

I will try to the best of my ability to tell you step-by-step what I saw and felt. Some of the things I did not understand. The Lord Jesus told me the meaning of most of them, but some things He did not tell me.

I knew then, and I know now, that these things were really happening and only God could have shown them to me. Praise His holy name. People, believe me, hell is real. I was taken there by the Spirit many times during the preparation of this report.

Soon we were high into the heavens. I turned and looked at Jesus. He was full of glory and power, and such peace flowed from Him. He took my hand and said, "I love you. Fear not, for I am with you."

At that, we began to go even higher into the sky, and now I could see the earth below. Protruding out of the earth and scattered about in many places were funnels spinning around to a center point and then turning back again. These moved high above the earth and looked like a giant, dirty type of slinky that moved continuously. They were coming up from all over the earth. "What are these?" I asked the Lord Jesus as we came near to one.

"These are the gateways to hell," He said. "We will go into hell through one of them."

Immediately, we entered one of the funnels. Inside, it looked like a tunnel, spinning around and around and back again like a top.

A deep darkness descended on us, and with the darkness came a smell so horrible it took my breath away. Along the sides of this tunnel were living forms embedded in the walls. Dark gray in color, the forms moved and cried out to us as we passed. I knew without being told that they were evil.

The forms could move but were still attached to the walls. A horrible smell came from them, and they screeched at us with the most awful cries. I felt an invisible, evil force moving inside the tunnels.

At times in the darkness, I could make out the forms. A dirty fog covered most of them. "Lord, what are these?" I asked as I held on tightly to Jesus' hand.

He said, "These are evil spirits ready to be spewed out on the earth when Satan gives the orders."

As we were going down inside the tunnel, the evil forms laughed and called out to us. They tried to touch us, but could not because of the power of Jesus. The very air was polluted and dirty, and only the presence of Jesus kept me from screaming at the sheer horror.

Oh, yes, I had all my senses—I could hear, smell, see, feel and even taste the evil in this place. If anything, my senses had become more sensitive, and the odor and filth almost made me sick.

Screams filled the air as we came near the base of the tunnel. Piercing cries came up the dark tunnel to meet us. Sounds of all sorts filled the air. I could feel fear, death and sin all around me.

The worst odor I have ever smelled filled the air. It was the smell of decaying flesh, and it seemed to be coming from every direction. Never on earth had I felt such evil or heard such cries of despair. Soon I would find that these were the cries of the dead and that hell was filled with their wails.

I felt a gust of evil wind and a small suction force ahead of us. Lights like lightening or strobe flashes penetrated the black darkness and threw gray shadows on the walls. I could barely make out the form of something in front of me. I recoiled in shock when I realized that it was a large snake moving along ahead of us. As I continued to look, I saw those ugly snakes were slithering about everywhere.

Jesus said to me, "We will soon enter the left leg of hell. Ahead you will see great sorrow, pathetic sadness and indescribable horror. Stay close to Me, and I will give you strength and protection as we go through hell.

"The things you are about to see are a warning," He said. "The book you write will save many souls from hell. What you are seeing is real. Fear not, for I will be with you."

At long last, the Lord Jesus and I were at the bottom of the tunnel. We stepped out into hell. I will try to the best of my ability to tell you what I saw, and I will tell it in the order God gave it to me.

Ahead of us, as far as I could see, were flying objects darting here and there. Groaning sounds and pitiful cries filled the air. Up ahead I saw a dim light, and we began walking toward it. The path was a dry, powdery dirt. We were soon at the entrance to a small dark tunnel.

Some things I cannot put on paper; they were too awful to describe. The fear in hell could be tasted, and I knew if I had not been with Jesus I would not make it back. In the writing of this, some of the things I saw I do not understand, but the

Lord knows all things, and He helped me understand most of what I saw.

Let me warn you—don't go to that place. It is a horrid place of torments, excruciating pain and eternal sorrow. Your soul will always be alive. The soul lives forever. It is the real you, and your soul will go to either heaven or hell.

To those of you who think that hell is here on earth—well, you are right—it is! Hell is in the center of the earth, and there are souls in torment there night and day. There are no parties in hell. No love. No compassion. No rest. Only a place of sorrow beyond your belief.

2

The Left Leg of Hell

A horrible odor filled the air. Jesus said to me, "In the left leg of hell are many pits. This tunnel branches off into other parts of hell, but we will spend some time in the left leg first.

"These things you are about to see will always be with you. The world must know about the reality of hell. Many sinners and even some of My people do not believe that hell is real. You have been chosen by Me to reveal these truths to them. Everything I will show you about hell and all the other things I will show you are true."

Jesus had shown Himself to me in the form of a bright light, brighter than the sun. The form of a man was in the center of that light. Sometimes I saw Jesus as a man, but at other times He was in the form of a spirit.

21

He spoke again, "Child, when I speak, the Father has spoken. The Father and I are one. Remember to love above all else and to forgive one another. Come now, follow Me."

As we walked, evil spirits fled from the presence of the Lord. "O God, O God," I cried. "What is next?"

As I said previously, I had all my senses in hell. All those in hell have all their senses. Mine were working now in full force. Fear was on every side, and inexpressible dangers lurked everywhere. Each step I took was more horrible than the one before.

There were doorways about the size of small windows, opening and shutting very fast at the top of the tunnel. Screams filled the air as many evil creatures flew by us, up and out of the gateways of hell. Soon we were at the end of the tunnel. I was trembling with fright because of the danger and fear around us.

I was so thankful for the protection of Jesus. I thank God for His almighty power to protect us, even in the pits of hell. Even with that protecting shield, I kept thinking, Not my will, Father, but Yours be done.

I looked at my body. For the first time I noticed that I was in a spirit form, and my form was in the shape of myself. I wondered what was next.

Jesus and I stepped from the tunnel onto a path with wide swaths of land on each side of it. There were pits of fire everywhere as far as the eye could see. The pits were four feet across and three feet deep and shaped like a bowl. Jesus said, "There are many pits like this in the left leg of hell. Come, I will show you some of them."

I stood beside Jesus on the path and looked into one of the pits. Brimstone was embedded in the side of the pit and glowed red like hot coals of fire. In the center of the pit was a lost soul who had died and gone to hell. Fire began at the bottom of the pit, swept upward and clothed the lost soul in flames. In a moment the fire would die down to embers, then with a rushing sound would sweep back over the tormented soul in the pit.

I looked and saw that the lost soul in the pit was caged inside a skeleton form. "My Lord," I cried at the sight, "Can't you let them out?" How awful was the sight! I thought, This could be me. I said, "Lord, how sad it is to see and know that a living soul is in there."

I heard a cry from the center of the first pit. I saw a soul in the form of a skeleton, crying, "Jesus, have mercy!"

"O, Lord!" I said. It was the voice of a woman. I looked at her and wanted to pull her out of the fire. The sight of her broke my heart.

The skeleton form of a woman with a dirty-grey mist inside was talking to Jesus. In shock, I listened to her. Decayed flesh hung by shreds from her bones, and, as it burned, it fell off into the bottom of the pit. Where her eyes had once been were now only empty sockets. She had no hair.

The fire started at her feet in small flames and grew as it climbed up and over her body. The woman seemed to be constantly burning, even when the flames were only embers. From deep down inside her came cries and groans of despair, "Lord, Lord, I want out of here!"

She kept reaching out to Jesus. I looked at Jesus, and there was great sorrow on His face. Jesus said to me, "My child, you are here with Me to let the world know that sin results in death, that hell is real."

I looked at the woman again, and worms were crawling out of the bones of her skeleton. They were not harmed by the fire. Jesus said, "She knows and feels those worms inside."

"God, have mercy!" I cried as the fire reached its peak and the horrible burning started all over again. Great cries and deep sobs shook the form of this woman-soul. She was lost. There was no way out. "Jesus, why is she here?" I said in a small voice, for I was very scared.

Jesus said, "Come."

The path we were on was a circuitous one, twisting in and out between these pits of fire as far as I could see. The cries of the living dead, mixed with moans and hideous screams, came to my ears from all directions. There were no quiet times in hell. The smell of dead and decaying flesh hung thickly in the air.

We came to the next pit. Inside this pit, which was the same size as the other one, was another skeleton form. A man's voice cried from the pit, saying, "Lord, have mercy on me!" Only when they spoke could I tell whether the soul was a man or woman.

Great wailing sobs came from this man. "I'm so sorry, Jesus. Forgive me. Take me out of here. I have been in this place of torment for years. I beg You, let me out!" Great sobs shook his skeletal frame as he begged, "Please, Jesus, let me out!" I looked at Jesus and saw that He too was crying.

"Lord Jesus," the man cried out from the burning pit, "haven't I suffered enough for my sins? It has been forty years since my death."

Jesus said, "It is written, *'The just shall live by faith!'* All mockers and unbelievers shall have their part in the lake of fire. You would not believe the truth. Many times My people were sent to you to show you the way, but you would not listen to them. You laughed at them and refused the gospel. Even though I died on a cross for you, you mocked Me and would not repent of your sins. My Father gave you many opportunities to be saved. If only you had listened!" Jesus wept.

"I know, Lord, I know!" the man cried. "But I repent now."

"It is too late," said Jesus. "Judgment is set."

The man continued, "Lord, some of my people are coming here, for they also will not repent. Please, Lord, let me go tell them that they must repent of their sins while they are still on earth. I do not want them to come here."

Jesus said, "They have preachers, teachers, elders—all ministering the gospel. They will tell them. They also have the advantages of the modern communications systems and many other ways to learn of Me. I sent workers to them that they might believe and be saved. If they will not believe when they hear the gospel, neither will they be persuaded though one rises from the dead."

At this, the man became very angry and began to curse. Evil, blasphemous words came from him. I looked on in horror as the flames rose up and his dead, decaying flesh began to burn and fall off. Inside this dead shell of a man, I saw his soul. It looked like a dirty-gray mist, and it filled the inside of his skeleton.

I turned to Jesus and cried, "Lord, how horrible!"

Jesus said, "Hell is real; the judgment is real. I love them so, My child. This is only the beginning of the frightful things I have to show you. There is much more to come.

"Tell the world for Me that hell is real, that men and women must repent of their sins. Come, follow Me. We must go on."

In the next pit was a very small-framed woman who looked to be about eighty years old. I can't say how I knew her age, but I did. The skin was removed from her bones by the continual flame, and only the bones remained with a dirty-mist soul inside. I watched as the fire burned her. Soon there were only the bones and the worms crawling inside, which the fire could not burn.

"Lord, how terrible!" I cried. "I don't know if I can go on, for this is awful beyond belief." As far as my eyes could see, souls were burning in pits of fire.

"My child, this is why you are here," Jesus answered. "You must know and tell the truth about hell. Heaven is real! Hell is real! Come, we must go on."

I looked back at the woman. Her cries were so sad. As I watched her, she put her bony hands together, as if in prayer. I couldn't help crying. I was in a spirit form, and I was crying. I knew that people in hell felt all these things, too.

Jesus knew my thoughts. "Yes, child," He said, "they do. When people come here, they have the same feelings and thoughts as when they were on earth. They remember their families and friends and all the times they had a chance to repent but refused to do so. Memory is always with them. If only they had believed the gospel and repented before it was too late."

I looked at the old woman once again, and this time I noticed that she had only one leg, and there seemed to be holes drilled in her hip bones. "What are these, Jesus?" I asked.

He said, "Child, while she was on earth, she had cancer and was in much pain. Surgery was done to save her life. She lay a bitter old woman for many years. Many of My people came to pray for her and to tell her I could heal her. She said, 'God did this to me,' and she would not repent and believe the gospel. She even knew Me once, but in time she came to hate Me.

"She said she did not need God and did not want Me to heal her. Yet I pleaded with her, still wanting to help her, wanting to heal and to bless her. She turned her back on Me and cursed Me. She said she did not want Me. My spirit pleaded with her. Even after she had turned her back on Me, I still tried to draw her by My spirit, but she would not listen. At last she died and came here."

The old woman cried out to Jesus, "Lord Jesus, please forgive me now. I'm sorry that I didn't repent while I was on earth." With great sobs she cried out to Jesus, "If only I had repented before it was too late! Lord, help me out of here. I will serve You. I will be good. Haven't I suffered enough? Why did I wait until too late? Oh, why did I wait until Your Spirit quit striving with me?"

Jesus said to her, "You had chance after chance to repent and serve Me." Sadness was written all over Jesus' face as we walked away.

As I watched the old woman cry, I asked, "Lord, what is next?"

I could feel fear all around. Sorrow, cries of pain and an atmosphere of death were everywhere. Jesus and I walked in grief and pity to the next pit. Only by His strength could I go on. For a great distance I could still hear the old woman's cries of repentance and pleading for forgiveness. If only there was something I could do to help her, I thought. Sinner, please don't wait until God's Spirit quits striving with you.

In the next pit was a woman on her knees, as if looking for something. Her skeletal form also was full of holes. Her bones were showing through, and her torn dress was on fire. Her head was bald, and there were only holes where her eyes and nose were supposed to be. A small fire was burning around her feet where she was kneeling, and she clawed the sides of the brimstone pit. The fire clung to her hands, and dead flesh kept falling off as she dug.

Tremendous sobs shook her. "O Lord, O Lord," she cried, "I want out." As we watched, she finally got to the top of the pit with her feet. I thought she was going to get out when a large demon with great wings that seemed to be broken at the top and hung down his sides ran to her. His color was brownish-black, and he had hair all over his large form. His eyes were set far back into his head, and he was about the size of a large grizzly bear. The demon rushed up to the woman and pushed her very hard backward into the pit and fire. I watched in horror as she fell. I felt so sorry for her. I wanted to take her into my arms and hold her, to ask God to heal her and take her out of there.

Jesus knew my thoughts and said, "My child, judgment has been set. God has spoken. Even when she was a child, I called and called her to repent and to serve Me. When she was sixteen years old, I came to her and said, 'I love you. Give your life to Me, and come follow Me, for I have called you for a special purpose.' I called all her life, but she would not listen. She said, 'Someday I will serve You. I have no time for You now. No time, no time, I have my life of fun. No time, no time to serve You, Jesus. Tomorrow I will.' Tomorrow never came, for she waited too long."

The woman cried out to Jesus, "My soul is truly in torment. There is no way out. I know that I wanted the world instead of You, Lord. I wanted riches, fame and fortune, and I got it. I could buy anything I wanted; I was my own boss. I was the prettiest, best-dressed woman of my time. And I had riches, fame and fortune, but I found I could not take them with me in death. O Lord, hell is horrible.

I have no rest day or night. I am always in pain and torment. Help me, Lord," she cried.

The woman looked up at Jesus so longingly and said, "My sweet Lord, if only I had listened to you! I will regret that forever. I planned to serve You someday—when I got ready. I thought You would always be there for me. But how wrong I was! I was one of the most sought-after women of my time for my beauty. I knew God was calling me to repent. All my life He drew me with cords of love, and I thought I could use God like I used everyone else. He would always be there. Oh yes, I used God! He would try so hard to get me to serve Him, while all the time I thought I didn't need Him. Oh, how wrong I was! For Satan began to use me, and I began to serve Satan more and more. At the last I loved him more than God. I loved to sin and would not turn to God.

"Satan used my beauty and my money, and all my thoughts turned to how much power he would give me. Even then, God continued to draw me. But I thought, I have tomorrow or the next day. Then one day while riding in a car, my driver ran into a house, and I was killed. Lord, please let me out." As she spoke her bony hands and arms reached out to Jesus while the flames continued to burn her.

33

Jesus said, "The judgment is set."

Tears fell down His cheeks as we moved to the next pit. I was crying inside about the horrors of hell. "Dear Lord," I cried, "the torment is too real. When a soul comes here, there is no hope, no life, no love. Hell is too real." No way out, I thought. She must burn forever in these flames.

"Time is running out," Jesus said. "We will come back tomorrow."

Friend, if you are living in sin, please repent. If you have been born again and have turned your back on God, repent and turn back to Him now. Live good and stand for truth. Wake up before it is too late, and you can spend forever with the Lord in heaven.

Jesus spoke again, "Hell has a body (like a human form) lying on her back in the center of the earth. Hell is shaped like a human body— very large and with many chambers of torment.

"Remember to tell the people of earth that hell is real. Millions of lost souls are here, and more are coming every day. On the Great Judgment Day, death and hell will be cast into the lake of fire; that will be the second death."

3

The Right Leg of Hell

I had not been able to sleep or eat since I was in hell the night before. Each day I relived hell. When I closed my eyes, all I could see was hell. My ears could not shut out the cries of the damned. Just like a television program, I relived all the things I had witnessed in hell over and over. Each night I was in hell, and each day I labored to find just the right words to bring this frightful thing to all the world.

Jesus appeared to me again and said, "Tonight we are going into the right leg of hell, My child. Don't be frightened, for I love you and I am with you."

The face of the Lord was sorrowful, and His eyes were filled with great tenderness and deep love. Though those in hell were forever lost, I knew that He still loved them and would for all eternity.

"My child," He said, "God, our Father, gave each one of us a will so that we could choose whether we would serve Him or Satan. You see, God did not make hell for His people. Satan deceives many into following him, but hell was made for Satan and his angels. It is not My desire, nor that of My Father, that anyone should perish." Tears of compassion ran down Jesus' cheeks.

He began to speak again, "Remember My words in the days ahead as I show you hell: *'I have all power in heaven and earth.'* Now, at times it will seem to you that I have left you, but I have not. Also, at times we will be seen by the evil forces and lost souls, while at other times we will not be. No matter where we go, be at peace and fear not to follow Me."

We went on together. I followed closely behind Him crying. For days I had been crying, and I could not shake off the very presence of hell which was ever before me. I cried mostly inside. My spirit was very sad.

We arrived at the right leg of hell. Looking ahead, I saw that we were on a pathway which was dry and burned. Screams filled the dirty air, and the stench of death was everywhere. The odor was sometimes so repugnant that it made me sick to my stomach. Everywhere was darkness except for the light which emanated from Christ and the flaming pits, which dotted the landscape as far as I could see.

All at once, demons of all kinds were going past us. Imps growled at us as they went by. Demon spirits of all sizes and shapes were talking to each other. Out ahead of us, a big demon was giving orders to small ones. We stopped to listen, and Jesus said, "There is also an invisible army of evil forces that we do not see here—demons such as evil spirits of sickness."

"Go!" the larger demon said to the smaller imps and devils. "Do many evil things. Break up homes and destroy families. Seduce weak Christians, and misinstruct and mislead as many as you can. You shall have your reward when you return.

"Remember, you must be careful of those who have genuinely accepted Jesus as their Savior. They have the power to cast you out. Go now across the earth. I have lots of others up there already and still have others to send. Remember, we are servants of the prince of darkness and of the powers of the air."

At that, the evil forms began to flee up and out of hell. Doors in the top of the right leg of hell opened and shut very fast to let them out. Also, some went up and out the funnel we had come down.

I will try to describe the looks of these evil beings. The one speaking was very large, about the size of a full-grown grizzly bear, brown in color, with a head like a bat and eyes that were set very far back into a hairy face. Hairy arms fell to his sides, and fangs came out of the hair on his face.

Another one was small like a monkey with very long arms and with hair all over his body. His face was tiny, and he had a pointed nose. I could see no eyes on him anywhere.

Still another had a large head, large ears and a long tail, while yet one more was as large as a horse and had smooth skin. The sight of these demons and evil spirits, and the terrible odor that came from them, made me sick to my stomach. Everywhere I looked were demons and devils. The biggest of these demons, I learned from the Lord, were getting their orders straight from Satan.

Jesus and I walked on down the pathway until we came to another pit. Cries of pain, unforgettably sorrowful sounds, were everywhere. My Lord, what is next? I thought.

We walked directly past some of the evil beings, which didn't seem to see us, and stopped at another pit of fire and brimstone. In this next pit was a large-framed man. I heard him preaching the gospel. I looked in amazement to Jesus for an answer, for He always knew my thoughts. He said, "While he was on earth, this man was a preacher of the gospel. At one time he spoke the truth and served me."

I wondered what this man was doing in hell. He was about six feet tall, and his skeleton was a dirty, grayish color, like a tombstone. Parts of his clothing still hung on him. I wondered why the flames had left these torn and tattered clothes and had not burned them up. Burning flesh was hanging from him, and his skull seemed to be in flames. A terrible odor came from him.

I watched the man spread his hands as if he were holding a book and begin to read Scriptures from the make-believe book. Again, I remembered what Jesus had said: "You have all your senses in hell, and they are a lot stronger here."

The man read Scripture after Scripture, and I thought it was good. Jesus said to the man with great love in His voice, "Peace, be still." Immediately, the man stopped talking and turned slowly to look at Jesus.

I saw the man's soul inside this skeletal form. He said to the Lord, "Lord, now I will preach the truth to all the people. Now, Lord, I'm ready to go and tell others about this place. I know that while I was on earth, I didn't believe there was a hell, nor did I believe You were coming again. It was what people wanted to hear, and I compromised the truth to the people in my church.

"I know I didn't like anyone who was different in race or color of skin, and I caused many to fall away from You. I made my own rules about heaven and right and wrong. I know that I led many astray, and I caused many to stumble over Your Holy Word, and I took money from the poor. But, Lord, let me out, and I will do right. I won't take money from the church anymore. I have repented already. I will love people of every race and color."

Jesus said, "You not only distorted and misrepresented the Holy Word of God, but you lied about your not knowing the truth. The pleasures of life were more important to you than truth. I visited you Myself and tried to turn you around, but you would not listen. You went on your own way, and evil was your lord. You knew the truth, but you would not repent or turn back to Me. I was there all the time. I waited for you. I wanted you to repent, but you did not. And now the judgment has been set."

Pity was on the face of Jesus. I knew that if the man had listened to the Savior's call, he would not be here now. O people, please listen.

Jesus spoke to the backslider again, "You should have told the truth, and you would have turned many to righteousness with God's Word, which says that all unbelievers will have their part in the lake that burns with fire and brimstone.

"You knew the way of the cross. You knew the way of righteousness. You knew to speak the truth. But Satan filled your heart with lies, and you went into sin. You should have repented with sincerity, not halfway. My Word is true. It does not lie. And now it is too late, too late." At that, the man shook his fist at Jesus and cursed Him.

With sorrow, Jesus and I walked on to the next pit. The backslidden preacher was still cursing and angry at Jesus. As we walked past the pits of fire, the hands of the lost reached out to Jesus, and in pleading voices they called out to Him for mercy. Their bony hands and arms were gray-black from the burning—no live flesh or blood, no organs, only death and dying. Inside myself I was crying, O earth, repent. If you don't, you'll come here. Stop before it is too late.

We stopped at another pit. I felt such pity for all of them and such sorrow that I was physically weak and could hardly stand. Great sobs shook me. "Jesus, I hurt so inside," I said.

From the pit a woman's voice spoke to Jesus. She stood in the center of the flames, and they covered her whole body. Her bones were full of worms and dead flesh. As the flames flickered up around her, she raised her hands towards Jesus, crying, "Let me out of here. I will give You my heart now, Jesus. I will tell others about Your forgiveness. I will witness for You. I beg You, please let me out!"

Jesus said, "My Word is true, and it declares that all must repent and turn from their sins and ask Me to come into their lives if they are to escape this place. Through My blood there is forgiveness of sins. I am faithful and just and will forgive all those who come to Me. I will not cast them out."

He turned, looked at the woman and said, "If you had listened to Me and had come to Me and repented, I would have forgiven you."

The woman asked, "Lord, is there no way out of here?"

Jesus spoke very softly. "Woman," He said, "you were given many opportunities to repent, but you hardened your heart and would not. And you knew My Word said that all whoremongers will have their part in the lake of fire."

Jesus turned to me and said, "This woman had sinful affairs with many men, and she caused many homes to be broken apart. Yet through all this, I loved her still. I came to her not in condemnation but with salvation. I sent many of My servants to her that she might repent of her evil ways, but she would not. When she was a young woman, I called her, but she continued to do evil. She did many wrongs, yet I would have forgiven her if she had come to Me. Satan entered into her, and she grew bitter and would not forgive others.

"She went to church just to get men. She found them and seduced them. If she had only come to Me, her sins would all have been washed away by My blood. Part of her wanted to serve Me, but you cannot serve God and Satan at the same time. Every person must make a choice as to whom they will serve."

"Lord," I cried, "give me strength to go on." I was shaking from my head to my feet because of the horrors of hell.

Jesus said to me, "Peace, be still."

"Help me, Lord," I cried. "Satan doesn't want us to know the truth about hell. In all my wildest dreams, I never thought that hell would be like this. Dear Jesus, when will this end?"

"My child," Jesus replied, "only the Father knows when the end will come." Then He spoke to me again and said, "Peace, be still." Great strength came upon me.

Jesus and I walked on through the pits. I wanted to pull each person I passed from the fire and rush them to the feet of Jesus. I wept much inside. I thought to myself, I never want my children to come here.

At last, Jesus turned to me and said quietly, "My child, we will go to your home now. Tomorrow night we shall return to this part of hell."

Back at my home I cried and cried. During the day I relived hell and the horror of all those people there. I told everyone I met during the day about hell. I told them that the pain of hell is beyond belief.

Those of you who read this book, please, I beg of you, repent of your sins. Call on Jesus and ask Him to save you. Call on Him today. Do not wait until tomorrow. Tomorrow may not come. Time is quickly running out. Fall on your knees and be cleansed from your sins. Be good to each other. For Jesus' sake, be kind and forgiving to one another.

If you are angry with someone, forgive him. No anger is worth going to hell for. Be forgiving as Christ forgives us of our sins. Jesus is able to keep us if we have a repentant heart and will let His blood cleanse us from all sin. Love your children, and love your neighbor as yourself.

The Lord of the churches says, "Repent and be saved!"

4

More Pits

The next night Jesus and I went again into the right leg of hell. I saw as before the love Jesus had for the souls that are lost in hell. And I felt His love for me and for all those who were on earth.

"Child," He said to me, "it is not the Father's will that anyone perish. Satan deceives many, and they follow him. But God is forgiving. He is a God of love. If these had truly come unto the Father and repented, He would have forgiven them." Great tenderness covered Jesus' face as He spoke.

Again we walked among the flaming pits and passed by more people in the torments I described earlier. My Lord, my Lord, such horrors! I thought. On and on we walked past many, many souls burning in hell.

All along the pathway burning hands reached out to Jesus. There were only bones where the flesh should have been—a grayish mass with burning and decayed flesh hanging in shreds. Inside each frame of their skeleton form was a dirty-gray mist-soul caught inside a dry skeleton forever. I could tell by their cries that they felt the fire, the worms, the pain, the hopelessness. And their cries filled my soul with a grief so great I cannot describe it. If only they had listened, I thought, they would not be here.

I knew that the lost in hell had all their senses. They remembered all that was ever told them. They knew there was no way out of the flames and that they were lost forever. Yet, without hope, they still hoped as they cried out to Jesus for mercy.

We stopped at the next pit. It was exactly like all the others. Inside it was the form of a woman, which I knew by her voice. She cried out to Jesus for deliverance from the flames.

Jesus looked on the woman with love and said, "While you were on earth, I called you to come to Me. I pleaded with you to get your heart right with Me before it was too late. I visited you many times in the midnight hour to tell you of My love. I wooed you, loved you and drew you to Me by My Spirit.

"'Yes Lord,' you said, 'I will follow You,' With your lips you said you loved Me, but your heart did not mean it. I knew where your heart was. I often sent my messengers to you to tell you to repent of your sins and come to Me, but you would not hear Me. I wanted to use you to minister to others, to help others to find Me. But you wanted the world and not Me. I called you, but you would not hear Me, nor would you repent of your sins."

The woman said to Jesus, "You remember, Lord, how I went to church and was a good woman. I joined the church. I was a member of Your church. I knew Your call was on my life. I knew I had to obey that call at all costs, and I did."

Jesus said, "Woman, you are still full of lies and sin. I called you, but you would not hear Me! True, you were a member of a church, but being a church member did not get you to heaven. Your sins were many, and you did not repent. You caused others to stumble at My Word. You would not forgive others when they hurt you. You pretended to love and serve Me when you were with Christians, but when you were away from Christians, you lied, cheated and stole. You gave heed to seducing spirits and enjoyed your double life. You knew the straight and narrow way."

"And," Jesus said, "you also had a double tongue. You talked about your brothers and sisters in Christ. You judged them and thought you were holier than they, when there was gross sin in your heart. This I know, you would not listen to My sweet Spirit of compassion. You judged the outside of a person, without regard to the fact that many were children in the faith. You were very hard.

"Yes, you said you loved Me with your lips, but your heart was far from Me. You knew the ways of the Lord and you understood. You played with God, and God knows all things. If you had sincerely served God, you would not be here today. You cannot serve Satan and God at the same time."

Jesus turned to me and said, "Many in the last days will depart from the faith, giving heed to seducing spirits and will serve sin. Come out from among them, and be separate. Walk not in the way with them." As we walked away, the woman began to curse and swear at Jesus. She screamed and cried with rage. We walked on. I was so weak in body.

In the next pit was the form of another skeleton. I smelled the odor of death even before we arrived. This skeleton looked the same as the others.

I wondered what this soul had done that it should be lost and hopeless, with no future except an eternity in this dreadful place. Hell is for eternity. As I heard the crying of the souls in torment, I cried too.

I listened as a woman spoke to Jesus from the flames of the pit. She was quoting the Word of God. "Dear Lord, what is she doing here?" I asked.

"Listen," said Jesus.

The woman said, "Jesus is the Way, the Truth and the Life. No man comes to the Father but by Him. Jesus is the Light of the World. Come to Jesus, and He will save you."

When she spoke, many of the lost souls around her listened. Some swore and cursed at her. Some told her to stop. Still others said, "Is there really hope?" or "Help us, Jesus." Great cries of sorrow filled the air.

I didn't understand what was happening. I did not know why the woman was preaching the gospel here.

The Lord knew my thoughts. He said, "Child, I called this woman at the age of thirty to preach My Word and to be a witness of the gospel. I call different ones for different purposes in My body. But if man or woman, boy or girl doesn't want My Spirit, I will depart.

"Yes, she did answer My call for many years, and she grew in the knowledge of the Lord. She learned My voice, and she did many good works for Me. She studied the Word of God. She prayed often, and she had many prayers answered. She taught many people the way of holiness. She was faithful in her house.

"The years went by until one day she found out that her husband was having an affair with another woman. And even though he asked for forgiveness, she grew bitter and would not forgive him and try to save her marriage. True, her husband was wrong, and he did commit a very grave sin.

"But this woman knew My Word. She knew to forgive, and she knew that with every temptation there is a way of escape. Her husband asked her to forgive him. She would not. Instead, anger took root. Anger grew inside her. She would not turn it over to Me. She turned more bitter each day and said in her heart, Here I am serving God all the way, and my husband is running around with another woman! 'Do you think that is right?' She said to Me.

"I said, 'No, it is not right. But he came to you and repented and said he would never do that again.'

"I told her, 'Daughter, look inside yourself, and see that you have caused this yourself.'

"'Not me, Lord,' she said, 'I am the holy one, and he is the sinful one.' She would not listen to Me.

"Time went on, and she wouldn't pray to Me or read the Bible. She became angry not only at her husband, but also at those around her. She quoted the Scriptures, but she would not forgive him.

"She would not listen to Me. Her heart grew bitter, and great sin entered in. Murder grew in her heart where love had once been. And one day, in her anger, she killed her husband and the other woman. Satan then took her over completely, and she killed herself."

I looked at that lost soul that had given up Christ and condemned her soul forever to the flames and the pain. I listened as she responded to Jesus. "I will forgive now, Lord," she said. "Let me out. I will obey You now. See, Lord, I am preaching Your Word now. In an hour demons will come to take me to be tormented even worse. For hours they will torture me. Because I was preaching your Word, my torments are worse. Please, Lord, I beg You to let me out."

I cried with the woman in the pit and asked the Lord to please keep me from all bitterness of heart. "Don't let me allow hatred to come into my heart, Lord Jesus," I said.

"Come, let us go on," Jesus said.

In the next pit was the soul of a man wrapped in its skeleton form, crying out to Jesus. "Lord," he cried, "help me to understand why I am here."

Jesus said, "Peace, be still. You understand why you are here."

"Let me out, and I will be good," the man begged.

The Lord said to him, "Even in hell you are still lying."

Jesus then turned to me and said, "This man was 23 years old when he came here. He would not listen to My gospel. He heard My Word many times and was often in My house. I drew him by My Spirit unto salvation, but he wanted the world and its lust. He liked to drink and would not heed My call. He was raised in the church, but he would not commit himself to Me. One day he said to Me, 'I will give my life to You one day, Jesus.' But that day never came. One night after a party, he was in a car wreck and was killed. Satan deceived him to the very end.

"He was killed instantly. He would not listen to My call. Others were also killed in the accident. Satan's work is to kill, steal and destroy. If only this young man had listened! It is not the Father's will that any perish. Satan wanted this man's soul, and he destroyed it through carelessness, sin and strong drink. Many homes and lives are destroyed every year because of alcohol."

If people could only see that the lusts and desires of the world are only for a season! If you come to the Lord Jesus, He will deliver you from strong drink. Call on Jesus, and He will hear you and help you. He will be your friend. Remember He loves you, and He also has the power to forgive your sins.

Married Christians, Jesus warns that you must not commit adultery. And desiring someone of the opposite sex, even when you don't commit adultery, could be adultery in your heart.

Young people, stay away from drugs and sex sins. If you have sinned, God will forgive you. Call on Him now while there is still time. Find strong Christian adults, and ask them if you can talk with them about your problems. You will be glad that you took the time now in this world before it is too late.

Satan comes as an angel of light to deceive the world. No wonder the sins of the world look tempting to this young man, even though he knew God's Holy Word. One more party, he thought, Jesus will understand. But death has no mercy. He waited too late.

I looked at the soul of the man, and I was reminded of my own children. "Oh God, may they serve You!" I know that many of you who are reading this have loved ones, maybe children, that you do not want to go to hell. Tell them about Jesus before it is too late. Tell them to repent of their sins and that God will forgive them and make them holy.

The man's cries rang inside me for days. I will never forget his cries of regret. I remember the flesh hanging and burning in the flames. I cannot forget the decay, the smell of death, holes where eyes once were, the dirty-gray souls and the worms that crawled through the bones. The form of the young man raised his arms toward Jesus pleadingly as we walked away toward the next pit.

"Dear Lord," I prayed, "give me the strength to go on."

I heard a woman's voice crying out in desperation. Cries of the dead were everywhere.

Soon we came to the pit where the woman was. She was pleading with all her soul for Jesus to take her out of there. "Lord," she said, "haven't I been here long enough? My torment is more than I can bear. Please, Lord, let me out!" Sobs shook her form, and such pain was in her voice. I knew she was suffering greatly.

I said, "Jesus, is there nothing You can do?"

Jesus then spoke to the woman. "While you were on earth," He said, "I called and called for you to come to Me. I pleaded with you to get your heart

59

right with Me, to forgive others, to do right, to stay out of sin. I even visited you in the midnight hour and drew you by My Spirit time after time. With your lips you said you loved Me, but your heart was far from Me. Didn't you know that nothing can be hidden from God? You fooled others, but you could not fool Me. I sent still others to tell you to repent, but you would not listen. You would not hear, you would not see, and in anger you turned them away. I placed you where you could hear My Word. But you would not give your heart to Me.

"You were not sorry, nor were you ashamed of what you were doing. You hardened your heart and turned Me away. Now you are lost and forever undone. You should have listened to Me."

At this, she looked at Jesus and began to swear and to curse God. I felt the presence of evil spirits and knew that it was they who were cursing and swearing. How sad to be lost forever in hell! Resist the devil while you still may, and he will flee from you.

Jesus said, "The world and all that is in it will pass away, but my words will not pass away."

5

The Tunnel of Fear

I tried to remember the preaching I had heard about hell. But never had I heard about such dreadful things as the Lord had shown me here. Hell was infinitely worse than anyone could think or imagine. It hurt me so to know that the souls that are now in torment in hell will be there for eternity. There is no way out.

I am determined that I will do everything in my power to save souls from these horrors. I must preach the gospel to everyone I meet, for hell is a frightful place, and this is a true report. Do you realize what I am saying? If sinners do not repent and believe the gospel, they will surely end up here.

Believe in the Lord Jesus Christ, and call on Him to save you from sin. Read chapters 3 and 14 of the Gospel of John. And please read this book from cover to cover so you can understand more about hell and the hereafter. As you read, pray that Jesus will come into your heart and wash away your sins before it is too late.

Jesus and I walked on through hell. The pathway was burned, dry, cracked and barren ground. I looked down the rows of pits as far as I could see. I was very tired. My heart, my very spirit, was broken from all I had seen and heard and yet I knew that more was still ahead.

"Jesus, give me the strength to go on," I cried.

As Jesus led, I walked closely behind Him. I was filled with sorrow for all the awful things I had seen. I was wondering inside of me if the world would believe me. I looked to my left and to my right and behind me—there were pits of fire as far as I could see. I was encircled by the fire, the flames and the burning souls. I cried out in sheer terror. The horror and reality of what I was seeing was too much for me to bear.

"O earth, repent," I cried. Great sobs shook my spirit as I walked on with Jesus. I wondered what was next. I wondered what my family and friends were doing. Oh, how I loved them! I remembered how I had sinned before I had returned to Jesus, and I thanked God that I had come back before it was too late.

Jesus said, "We are now about to enter a tunnel which will take us into the belly of hell. Hell is shaped like a human body lying in the center of the earth. The body is lying on her back, with both arms and both legs stretched out. As I have a body of believers, so hell has a body of sin and death. As the Christ-body is built up daily, so the hell-body is also built up daily."

On our way to the tunnel, we walked on past the flaming pits with the cries and moans of the damned ringing in my ears. Many called out to Jesus as we went by. Others tried to climb out of the pits of fire in order to reach Him, but could not. Too late, too late, my heart cried.

Sorrow was always upon Jesus' face as we walked. I remember looking at the pits of fire and thinking about the many times we had had cookouts in our backyard and how the red hot coals looked when they had been smoldering for hours. It was so much like what I was seeing here in hell.

I was so thankful when we entered the tunnel. I thought, The tunnel cannot possibly be as bad as the pits. But how wrong I was!

As soon as we were inside, I began to see great snakes, large rats and many evil spirits, all running from the presence of the Lord. The snakes hissed at us, and the rats squealed. There were many evil sounds. Vipers and dark shadows were all about us. Jesus was the only light to be seen in the tunnel. I stayed as close to Him as I could.

Imps and devils were all over the sides of this cavern, and they were all going somewhere up and out of the tunnel. I found out later that these evil spirits were going out onto the earth to do Satan's bidding.

Feeling my fear of this dark, damp, dirty place, Jesus said, "Fear not; we will be at the end of the tunnel soon. I must show you these things. Come, follow Me."

Giant snakes slithered past us. Some of the snakes were as large as four feet around and 25 feet long. Dense, dirty odors filled the air, and evil spirits were everywhere.

Jesus spoke. "We will soon be to the belly of hell. This part of hell is seventeen miles high and three miles around like a circle." Jesus gave me the exact measurements.

I will try to the best of my ability to write and tell what I saw and heard. I will do it for the glory of the Father, the glory of the Son and the glory of the Holy Ghost. May the will of God be done.

I knew that Jesus was showing me all these things so that I could warn the men and women of the world to shun hell at all cost. Dear ones, if you are reading this and you do not know Jesus, stop right now, repent of your sins, and invite Him to be your Savior.

6

Activity in Hell

A head of us I could see a dim, yellow light. Jesus and I had come out of the tunnel of fear and now stood on a dirty ledge overlooking the belly of hell. As far as I could see, there was a great amount of activity going on in the center (the belly) of hell.

We stopped, and Jesus spoke. "I am going to take you through the belly of hell, and I am going to reveal many things to you. Come, follow Me." The two of us walked on.

Jesus said, "Ahead are many terrors. They are not the figment of someone's imagination—but they are real. Be sure to tell your readers that demon powers are real. Tell them also that Satan is real, and the powers of darkness are real. But tell them not to despair, for if My people which are called by My name will humble themselves and pray and turn from their wicked ways, then I will hear from heaven and heal their lands and their bodies. Just as surely as heaven is real—even so, hell is also real."

God wants you to know about hell, and He wants to save you from that place. God wants you to know you have a way out. That way is Jesus Christ, the Savior of your soul. Remember, only those with their names written in the Lamb's Book of Life will be saved.

We came to the first activity in the belly of hell. It was to the right of where we had entered and up on a small hill in a dark corner of hell.

I remembered the words of the Lord when He said to me, "It will seem sometimes like I have left you, but I will not. Remember that I have all power in heaven and in earth. At times the evil spirits and lost souls will not see us or know we are here. Fear not. What you are about to see is real. These things are happening right now and will continue to happen until death and hell are cast into the lake of fire."

Reader, make sure your name is written in the Lamb's Book of Life.

Ahead of us I could hear voices and the cries of a soul in torment. We walked up the small hill and looked over. A light filled the area, so I could see clearly. Cries like you have never thought possible were filling the air. They were the cries of a man.

"Listen to Me," said Jesus. "What you are about to see and hear is true. Take heed you ministers of the gospel, for these are faithful and true sayings. Awake, evangelists, preachers, and teachers of My Word, all of you who are called to preach the gospel of the Lord Jesus Christ. If you are sinning, repent or you will likewise perish."

We walked up to within fifteen feet of this activity. I saw small dark-clothed figures marching around a boxlike object. Upon closer examination, I saw that the box was a coffin and the figures marching around it were demons. It was a real coffin, and there were twelve demons marching around it. As they marched, they were chanting and laughing. Each one had a sharp spear in his hand, which he kept thrusting into the coffin through small openings that lined the outside.

There was a feeling of great fear in the air, and I trembled at the sight before me.

Jesus knew my thoughts, for He said, "Child, there are many souls in torment here, and there are many different types of torment for these souls. There is greater punishment for those who once preached the gospel and went back into sin, or for those who would not obey the call of God for their lives."

I heard a cry so desperate that it filled my heart with despair. "No hope, no hope!" he called. The hopeless cry came from the coffin. It was an endless wail of regret.

"Oh, how awful!" I said.

"Come," said Jesus, "let's go closer." With that, He walked up to the coffin and looked inside. I followed and also looked in. It appeared that the evil spirits could not see us.

A dirty-gray mist filled the inside of the coffin. It was the soul of a man. As I watched, the demons pushed their spears into the soul of the man in the coffin.

I will never forget the suffering of this soul. I cried to Jesus, "Let him out, Lord; let him out." The torment of his soul was such a terrible sight. If only he could get free. I pulled at Jesus' hand and begged Him to let the man out of the coffin.

Jesus said, "My child, peace, be still."

As Jesus spoke, the man saw us. He said, "Lord, Lord, let me out. Have mercy." I looked down and saw a bloody mess. Before my eyes was a soul. Inside the soul was a human heart, and blood spurted from it. The thrusting of the spears were literally piercing his heart.

"I will serve You now, Lord." He begged, "Please let me out." I knew that this man felt every spear that pierced his heart.

"Day and night, he is tormented," the Lord said. "He was put here by Satan, and it is Satan who torments him."

The man cried, "Lord, I will now preach the true gospel. I will tell about sin and hell. But please help me out of here."

Jesus said, "This man was a preacher of the Word of God. There was a time when he served Me with all his heart and led many people to salvation. Some of his converts are still serving Me today, many years later. The lust of the flesh and the deceitfulness of riches led him astray. He let Satan gain the rule over him. He had a big church, a fine car, a large income. He began to steal from the church offerings. He began to teach lies. He spoke mostly half-lies and half-truths. He would not let Me correct him. I sent My messengers to him to tell him to repent and preach the truth, but he loved the pleasures of this life more than the life of God. He knew not to teach or preach any other doctrine except the truth as revealed in the Bible. But before he died, he said the Holy Ghost baptism was a lie and that those who claimed to have the Holy Ghost were hypocrites. He said you could be a drunkard and get to heaven, even without repentance.

"He said God would not send anyone to hell —that God was too good to do that. He caused many good people to fall from the grace of the Lord. He even said that he did not need Me, for he was like a god. He went so far as to hold seminars to teach this false doctrine. He trampled My Holy Word under his feet. Yet, I continued to love him.

"My child, it is better to have never known Me than to know Me and turn back from serving Me," said the Lord.

"If only he had listened to You, Lord!" I cried. "If only he had cared about his soul and the souls of others."

"He did not listen to Me. When I called he would not hear Me. He loved the easy life. I called and called him to repentance, but he would not come back to Me. One day he was killed and came immediately here. Now Satan torments him for having once preached My Word and saved souls for My kingdom. This is his torment."

I watched the demons as they continued to march around and around the coffin. The man's heart beat and real blood ran from it. I will never forget his cries of pain and sorrow.

Jesus looked at the man in the coffin with great compassion and said, "The blood of many lost souls are upon this man's hands. Many of them are in torment here right now." With sorrowful hearts, Jesus and I walked on.

As we left, I saw another group of demons coming up to the coffin. They were about three feet high, dressed in black clothes, with black hoods over their faces. They were taking shifts tormenting this soul.

I thought of how pride in all of us at times makes us unwilling to admit mistakes and ask for forgiveness. We refuse to repent and humble ourselves, and we go on as if we alone were ever right. But listen, soul, hell is real. Please do not go to that place.

Then Jesus showed me a giant clock, stretched out across the whole world. And I heard it ticking. The hour hand was nearing the twelve o'clock position, and the minute hand raced around until it stopped at three minutes before twelve. Stealthily the minute hand moved toward the hour. As it moved, the ticking became louder and louder until it seemed to fill the whole earth.

God spoke like a trumpet, and His voice sounded like many waters. "Listen and hear what the Spirit is saying to the churches," He said. "Be ready, for at a time you think not, I will come again. I hear the clock striking. It is twelve o'clock. The Bridegroom has come for His bride."

Are you ready for Christ's coming, my friend? Or will you be like those who say, "Not today, Lord?" Will you call upon Him and be saved? Will you give your heart to Him today? Remember, Jesus can and will save you from all evil if you call on Him today and repent. Pray for your family and your loved ones that they will come to Christ before it is too late.

Listen as Jesus says, "I will protect you from evil. I will keep you in all your ways. I will save you. I will save your loved ones. Call upon Me today and live."

With many tears, I pray that all of you who read this book will realize the truth before it is too late. Hell is for eternity. I am trying to the best of my ability to reveal all I saw and heard. I know these things are true. As you read the remainder of this book, I pray that you will repent and take Jesus Christ as your personal Savior.

I heard the Lord say, "It is time to go. We shall return again tomorrow."

7

The Belly of Hell

The next night Jesus and I went into hell again. We entered first into a large open area. As far as I could see, evil activities were going on. A great number of these activities were centered around us. Only ten feet or so away from where we were standing, I noticed a peculiar activity—peculiar mainly because many evil forms and demon spirits hurried in and out of that particular area.

The scene was like something from a horror movie. As far as I could see, there were souls in torment, and the devil and his angels were going about their work. The semi-darkness was pierced with screams of agony and despair.

Jesus said, "Child, Satan is both the deceiver on earth and the tormentor of souls in hell. Many of the demonic powers seen here also go up on the earth at times to hurt, afflict and deceive. I am going to show you things that have never before been seen in this much detail. Some of the things you see will be happening now, while others are yet to happen in the future."

Again I looked ahead. The ground was a light brown in color, without life, without grass or anything green. Everything was dead or dying. Some places were cold and damp, while others were hot and dry. And always there was the putrid odor of burning and decaying flesh mingled with the smells of offal, stale garbage and mold.

"Satan uses many traps and snares to deceive God's people," Jesus said. "During our trips to hell, I will show you many of the cunning and insidious tricks of the devil."

We had walked only a few yards when I saw a dark, black object looming ominously ahead of us. It seemed to move up and down, to contract and to swell. And each time it moved it gave off an awful stench—an odor even greater than the usual, malodorous smells which filled the air of hell.

I will try to explain what I saw as best I can. As the large, hanging, black object continued to contract and expand and to breathe out offensive odors, I noticed something like horns, dark in color, coming out of it and going up into the earth. I realized that it was a large, black heart and that there were many entrances into it. A dreadful foreboding came over me.

Jesus knew my thoughts and said, "Fear not. This is the heart of hell. Later, we will go through it, but now we must go into the cell block of hell."

The cell block of hell was in a circle in the belly of hell. The cells are seventeen miles high. I looked up, and I saw there was a large brown ditch between the cells and the bottom or belly of hell. It looked to me like the ditch was about six feet deep, and I wondered how I was going to get across it. I had no sooner thought that than we were up on a ledge, at the first tier of cells. The ledge acted as a walkway around the cells and also as a vantage place from which one could look out over the center of hell.

Jesus said, "These things are faithful and true. Death and hell will one day be cast into the lake of fire. Until then, this is hell's holding place. These cells will continue to be here, packed with sinful souls, tormented and suffering.

"I gave My life so you would not have to come here. I knew these horrors were real, but My Father's mercy is just as real. If you will let Him, He will forgive you. Call to Him in My name today."

8

The Cells in Hell

Jesus and I stood on a ledge at the first tier of cells. The ledge was about four feet wide. I looked up, and as far as I could see, there were other ledges in a large circle around what looked like a giant pit. Beside the ledge, or walkway, were cells which had been dug into the earth. Like jail cells, these cells were all in a row, with only two feet of dirt separating them.

Jesus said, "This cell block is seventeen miles high, starting from the bottom of hell. Here in these cells are many souls that were in witchcraft or the occult. Some were sorcerers, mediums, drug peddlers, idol worshipers or evil people with familiar spirits. These are the souls that worked the greatest abominations against God—many of them have been here for hundreds of years. These are they who would not repent, especially those who deceived

81

people and led them away from God. These souls have done great wickedness against the Lord and His people. Evil and sin was their love and passion."

As I followed the Lord around the walkway, I looked down to the center of hell, where the greatest amount of activity was. A dim light filled the center at all times, and I could make out the movement of many forms. As far as I could see ahead of us were cells.

I thought to myself that the torment in the cells surely could not be more horrible than that in the pits. All around us I heard the cries and the moans and the screams of the damned in the cells. I began to be very sick. Great sorrow filled my heart.

Jesus said, "I did not let you hear those cries until now, child. But now I want to show you how Satan comes to steal, kill and destroy. Here in hell there are different torments for different souls. Satan administers this torment until the day of judgment, till death and hell are cast into the lake of fire. Also, a lake of fire comes through hell at times."

As we walked along the ledge, the sounds grew louder. Great cries came from inside the cells. As I walked close to Jesus, He stopped in front of the third cell. A bright light illumined the inside of the cell. In the cell was an old woman sitting in a rocking chair, rocking and crying as though her heart would break. I don't know why, but I was shocked to find that this woman was a real person with a body.

The cell was completely bare except for the woman in the rocking chair. The walls of the cell were constructed of light clay and dirt, molded into the earth. The front door spanned the entire front of the cell. It was made of black metal with bars of metal and a lock on it. Since the bars were set wide apart, Jesus and I had an almost unlimited view of the entire cell.

The old woman's color was ashen—flesh mixed with a grayish tint. She was rocking back and forth. As she rocked, tears rolled down her cheeks. I knew from her agonized expression that she was in great pain and was suffering from some unseen torment. I wondered what she had been charged with that she should be imprisoned here.

All of a sudden, right before my eyes, the woman began to change forms—first to an old, old man, then to a young woman, to a middle-aged woman and then back to the old lady I had first seen. In shock, I watched as she went through these changes one after the other.

When she saw Jesus, she cried, "Lord, have mercy on me. Let me out of this place of torment." She leaned forward in her chair and reached for Jesus, but could not get to Him. The changing continued. Even her clothes changed, so that she was attired as a man, then a young girl, a middle-aged woman and an old woman in turn. All of this changing seemed to take only a few minutes.

I asked Jesus, "Why, Lord?"

Again she screamed, "O Lord, let me out of here before they return." She now stood at the front of the cell, clenching the bars with tight fists. She said, "I know Your love is real. I know Your love is true. Let me out!" Then as the woman cried in terror, I saw that something was beginning to rip the flesh from her body.

"She is not what she appears to be," said the Lord.

The woman sat back in the chair and began to rock. But now only a skeleton was sitting in the rocking chair—a skeleton with a dirty mist inside. Where there had been a clothed body only minutes ago, now there were blackened and burned bones and empty sockets for eyes. The soul of the woman moaned and cried out to Jesus in repentance. But her cries were too late.

"Back on earth," said Jesus, "this woman was a witch and a worshiper of Satan. She not only practiced witchcraft, but she taught witchcraft to others. From the time she was a child, her family practiced the black arts. They loved darkness rather than light.

"Many times," said the Lord, "I called on her to repent. She mocked Me and said, 'I enjoy serving Satan. I will keep on serving him.' She rejected the truth and would not repent of her evil. She turned many people away from the Lord, some of them are in hell with her today. If she had repented, I would have saved her and many of her family, but she would not listen.

"Satan deceived this woman into believing that she would receive a kingdom of own as her reward for serving him. He told her she would never die, but would have a life with him forever. She died praising Satan and came here and asked him for her kingdom. Satan, the father of lies, laughed in her face and said, 'Did you think I would divide my kingdom with you? This is your kingdom.' And he locked her in this cell and torments her day and night.

"On earth this woman taught many witches, both white witches and black witches, to do their magic. One of her magical tricks was to change from a young woman, to a middle-aged woman, to an old woman—even to an old man. It was fun in those days to make the change and frighten lesser witches with her magic. But now she suffers the pains of hell, and her flesh is ripped away with each change. She cannot control it now, and keeps changing from one form to another, but her real form is the misty soul inside her skeleton. Satan uses her for his evil purposes and taunts and mocks her. Every so often she is brought back before Satan to be tormented for his pleasure.

"I called her many times, and I would have saved her. But she would not have Me. Now she begs and pleads for forgiveness, but it is too late. Now she is lost without hope."

I looked at this woman who was lost forever in suffering and pain, and though she was an evil woman, my heart was broken with compassion. "Lord, how awful!" I said in tears.

And then, just as if Jesus and I were not even there, a dirty, brown demon with broken wings, about the size and shape of a large bear, came to the front of her cell and opened it with a key. He was making a loud noise as if to frighten her. The woman screamed in abject terror as he began to attack her and pull her out of the cell.

Jesus said, "This demon torments her often." I watched as she was dragged out of the cell and taken away.

"Dear Lord," I asked, "is there nothing we can do?" I felt such a pity for her.

"It's too late!" Jesus replied. "It's too late."

9

The Horrors of Hell

I understand why the people in these cells in the belly of hell were different from those elsewhere in torment. There was much I did not understand. I simply listened to Jesus and made a record of all I heard and saw for the glory of God.

As far as I could see, the cells seemed to be in an endless circle. There was a single soul in each cell. Moans, wails, sighs and groans came from the cells as we walked past them.

We had not walked far when Jesus stopped in front of another cell. As we looked in, a light came on. (Jesus made the light.) I stood and looked at a soul that I knew was in great torment! It was another woman, and she was a blue-gray color. Her flesh was dead, and the parts that had decayed were falling off the bones. Her bones were all burned to a deep black, and she had on bits and pieces of ragged clothes. Worms were crawling out of her flesh and bones. A dirty odor filled the cell.

Like the woman before, she too was sitting in a rocking chair. She was holding a rag doll. And as she rocked, she cried and held the rag doll to her chest. Great sobs shook her body, and wailing cries came from the cell.

Jesus told me, "She also was a servant of Satan. She sold her soul to him, and while she was alive, she practiced every kind of evil. Witchcraft is real," said Jesus. "This woman taught and practiced witchcraft and turned many toward the path of sin. Those who were teachers of witchcraft received special attention and a greater amount of power from Satan than those who simply practiced it. She was a soothsayer, a diviner and a medium for her master.

"She gained great favor with Satan for all the evil she committed. She knew how to use the powers of darkness for herself and for Satan. She went to devil-worship services and praised Satan. She was a powerful woman for him."

I wondered how many souls she had deceived for Satan. I looked at this bony shell of a soul, crying over a rag doll—just a dirty piece of cloth. Sorrow filled my heart, and tears filled my eyes.

She held tightly to the rag doll as if it could help her, or perhaps she could help it. The smell of death filled the place.

Then I saw her begin to change like the other woman. She was first an old woman in the 1930's and then a young woman of today. Time after time, she made this fantastic transformation right before our eyes.

"This woman," said Jesus, "was the equivalent of a preacher for Satan. Just as the true gospel is preached to us by a real minister, so Satan has his counterfeit ministers. She had the strongest kind of satanic power, one which she was required to sell her soul to receive. Satan's evil gifts are like the opposite side of the coin to the spiritual gifts Jesus bestows upon believers. This is the power of darkness.

"These workers of Satan work in the occult, the witchcraft shops, as palm readers, and in many other ways. A medium of Satan is a powerful satanic worker. These individuals are utterly deceived and are sold out completely to Satan. Some workers of darkness cannot even speak to Satan unless their medium speaks for them. They make human and animal sacrifices to the devil.

"Many people give their souls to Satan. They choose to serve him instead of Me. Their choice is death unless they repent of their sins and call upon Me. I am faithful, and I will save them from their sins. Many also sell their souls to Satan thinking they will live forever. But they will die a horrible death.

"Satan still thinks he can overthrow God and disrupt God's plan, but he was defeated at the cross. I took the keys away from Satan, and I have all power in heaven and in earth.

"After this woman died, she went straight to hell. The demons brought her before Satan, where in anger she asked why the demons had control over her, for on earth she thought she controlled them. There they had done her bidding. She also asked Satan for the kingdom he had promised her.

"Satan kept on lying to her even after her death on earth. He said that he would restore her to life and use her for his purposes again. By deceit, she had gotten him many souls, so his lies sounded reasonable to her.

"But at the last, Satan had laughed and scorned her. He told her, 'I deceived you and used you all those years. I will never give you my kingdom.'"

The devil waved his arms at the woman, and it seemed that her flesh was being ripped from her bones. She screamed in pain as a large black book was brought for Satan. He opened it and ran his finger down the pages till he found her name.

"Oh, yes," Satan said, "you did serve me well on earth. You brought me more than 500 souls." He lied and said to her, "Your punishment will not be as bad as the others."

A cackle of evil laughter rang out. Satan stood and pointed a finger at the woman, and a great wind arose and filled the place. A sound like howling thunder rose from him.

"Ha-ha," said the devil, "get your kingdom if you can." Then an unseen force slammed her to the ground.

"You are going to serve me here also," Satan laughed as she tried to get up. The woman screamed in pain as the flesh continued to be ripped from her bones by demons.

She was dragged back to this cage. She remembered Satan's promises. He told her she would have all power. He told her she would never die. He told her he had power over life and death, and she had believed him. She was told that Satan could stop anything from killing her. Satan told her many lies and promised her many things.

Jesus said, "I came to save all men. I desire that all who are lost will repent and call upon My name. It is not My will that any should perish, but have everlasting life. Sad to say, most will not repent of their sins before they die, and they will go to hell. But the way to heaven is the same for all people. You must be born again to enter the kingdom of God. You must come to the Father in My name and repent of your sins. You must sincerely give your heart to God and serve Him. "

"Child," Jesus continued, "the next thing I will reveal to you is even more horrible. I know it will grieve you. Also, I want the world to hear and know what the Spirit is saying to the churches.

"In these cells, as far as you can see, are souls in torment. Each time the cells are filled, hell enlarges itself to receive even more souls. You have all your senses in hell. And if you were blind on earth, you will be blind in hell. If you had only one arm on earth, you will have only one arm in hell."

I must tell you to **repent**, for hell is a terrible place, a frightening place, a place of awful sadness and eternal cries of regret. Please, I beg you to believe what I say, for it is true. This was so difficult for me that I was sick many times during the preparing of this record.

I saw things in hell that are too horrible to tell —even more awful than the wails of torment, the odors of decaying flesh, and the dreadfulness of the fires of hell with its deep pits. I also saw things that God would not let me write.

When you die on earth, if you are born again by the Spirit of God, your soul goes to heaven. If you are a sinner when you die, you go immediately to a burning hell. Demons with great chains will drag your soul through the gateways of hell, where you will be thrown into the pits and tormented. In time, you will be brought before Satan. You know and feel all things that happen to you in hell.

Jesus told me that there is a place in hell called the "fun center." Souls confined to the pits cannot be brought there. He also told me that though torments are different for different souls, all are burned with fire.

The fun center is shaped like a circus arena. Several people who are to be the entertainment are brought to the center ring of the fun center. These are people who knowingly served Satan on earth. They are the ones who, of their own free will, chose to follow Satan instead of God. Around the sides of the arena are the other souls, except those from the pits.

The ones in the center ring were leaders in the occult world before their death. They were mediums, soothsayers, sorcerers, mind readers, witches and warlocks—all those who consciously made a choice to serve Satan.

When they were alive on earth, they deceived many and caused them to follow Satan and to sin. The ones who had been deceived and were caused to fall into sin came and tormented their deceivers. One by one they were allowed to torture them.

In one such torment, spiritual bones were taken apart and buried in different parts of hell. The soul was literally torn apart and the parts scattered across hell in a kind of demonic scavenger hunt. The mutilated souls felt tremendous pain. Those outside the arena could throw stones at those who were in the ring. Every imaginable method of torture was allowed. The souls being tormented cried out for death, but that is eternal death. Satan gave the orders for all this to be done. That is his fun center.

Jesus said, "I took the keys of hell away from Satan many years ago. I came and opened these cells and let My people out. For in the time of the Old Testament before I actually gave My life on the cross, paradise was situated close to hell. These cells were once in paradise; now Satan uses them for his evil purposes and has made more.

"O reader, will you repent of your sins before it is eternally too late? For all shall come before Me in the judgment. Paradise was moved from its position near hell when I died and rose again by the power of God, My Father."

Again, I will tell you that these cells, which are seventeen miles high, serve as a prison for those who once were Satan's workers of darkness, those involved with any kind of sin that had to do with demonic powers, the occult and satanic worship.

Jesus said, "Come, I want to show you something."

At once we were about a half-mile up in the air, in the center of the belly of hell, and in the center of the seventeen-mile-high block of cells. It felt like being in a well where neither top nor bottom could be seen because of the darkness. A yellow light began to fill the place. I held tight to Jesus' hand.

"Dear Lord," I asked, "why are we here?"

All at once there came a hurricane-force wind and a mighty rushing sound. Great waves of fire began to race up the sides of the walls of cells, burning everything in its path. The flames reached inside each cell and brought pitiful cries of pain and distress. Though Jesus and I were not touched by the flames, fear welled up inside of me as I saw the souls of the lost running to the back of the small cells, trying to find a hiding place.

An evil sound began to rise from the left of us. I looked, and Satan was standing with his back to us, and he was all aflame. But he was not being burned; rather, it was he who caused the fire. Now he stood engulfed in the flames, enjoying the cries of these poor, lost souls. As Satan moved his arms, great balls of fire shot from him.

Heartbreaking screams and great cries of pain came from the cells. The souls inside were being burned alive by this hotter than hot lake of fire, and yet they could not die. The demons, too, joined in the laughter as Satan went from cell to cell, torturing the lost.

Jesus said, "Satan feeds on evil. He glories in pain and suffering and gains power from it."

I watched Satan as a reddish-yellow flame with brown edges grew all about him. A wild and gusty wind blew his garments which did not burn. The smell of burning flesh filled the air, and I realized anew that the horrors of hell are real. Satan walked through the flames, and they could not burn him. Though I only saw his back, I could hear his evil laughter everywhere.

I watched as Satan ascended in a cloud of smoke, taking the stream of fire up with him to the top of the belly of hell. I listened as he turned and in a loud voice announced that unless all these souls worshiped him, he would give them a turn in the fun circle.

"No, please, Satan, we will worship you," they shouted in unison as they all began to bow in worship to the devil. And the more they worshiped him, the greater was his hunger for adoration. Louder and louder rang the sounds of praise until the rafters of hell rang with the clamor.

Jesus said, "All these who occupy the cells of hell heard the true gospel while they were alive on earth. Many times My salvation was offered to them. Many times My Spirit drew them, but they would not hearken or come unto Me to be saved."

As Jesus was speaking, Satan was saying to his subjects, "Ha-ha, this is your kingdom—all the kingdom you will ever have. My kingdom covers all the earth and the world below." I heard him shout, "This is your life for eternity!" While cries of regret came from the burning cells.

Jesus said, "My salvation is free. Whoever will, let him come and be saved from this place of everlasting punishment. I will not cast him out. If you have been a witch or a warlock, even if you have a written agreement with the devil, My power will break it, and My shed blood will save you. I will take the evil curse off your life and redeem you from hell. Give me your heart that I may unchain you and set you free."

10

The Heart of Hell

At night I went with Jesus into hell. During the day, hell was ever before my eyes. I tried to tell others about what I was seeing, but they would not believe me. I felt so very alone, and only by the grace of God could I go on. All glory belongs to the Lord Jesus Christ.

The next night Jesus and I went back to hell. We walked along the edge of the belly of hell. I recognized parts of it from being there before. The same rotting flesh, the same odor of evil, the same stale, hot air was everywhere. I was already very tired.

Jesus knew my thoughts and said, "I'll never leave or forsake you. I know you are weary, but I will strengthen you."

Jesus' touch did strengthen me, and we walked on. Ahead I saw a large black object, almost as big as a baseball field which seemed to be moving up and down. I remembered that I had been told this was "the heart of hell."

Coming out from this black heart were what looked like large arms or horns. They were coming out of it and going up and out of hell into the earth and over the earth. I wondered if these horns were the ones the Bible spoke about.

All around the heart, the earth was dry and brown. For about thirty feet in all directions, the earth had been burned and had dried to a rusty, brown color. The heart was the blackest of blacks, but another color like the scales of a snake's skin was intermixed with the black. An awful odor arose from the heart each time it beat. It moved as a real heart and beat up and down. An evil force field surrounded it.

In amazement I looked at this evil heart and wondered what was its purpose.

Jesus said, "These branches, which look like arteries of a heart, are pipelines that go up through the earth to spill out evil upon it. These are the horns that Daniel saw, and they represent evil kingdoms on the earth. Some have already been, some shall be, and some are now. Evil kingdoms will arise, and the Antichrist will rule over many peoples, places and things. If possible, the very elect will be deceived by him. Many will turn away and will worship the beast and his image.

"Out of these main branches or horns, smaller branches will grow. Out of the smaller branches will come demons, evil spirits and all manner of evil forces. They will be released upon the earth and instructed by Satan to do many evil works. These kingdoms and evil forces will obey the beast, and many will follow him to destruction. It is here in the heart of hell that these things begin."

These are the words that Jesus spoke to me. He instructed me to write them and put them into a book and to tell them to the world. These words are true. These revelations were given to me by the Lord Jesus Christ so that all may know and understand the workings of Satan and the evil schemes he is planning for the future.

Jesus said, "Follow me." We walked up a flight of stairs into the heart, where a doorway was opened before us. In the heart was total darkness. I heard the sounds of crying, and there was an odor so awful I could barely breathe. All I could see in the darkness was Jesus. I walked very close to Him.

And then, all of a sudden, Jesus was gone! The unthinkable had happened. I was alone in the heart of hell. Horror took hold of me. Fear gripped my soul, and death took hold of me.

I cried out to Jesus, "Where are You? Where are You? Oh, please come back, Lord!" I called and I called, but no one answered.

"O my God," I wailed, "I must get out of here." I began to run in the darkness. As I touched the walls, they seemed to breathe, moving against my hands. And then I was no longer alone.

I heard the sound of laughter as two demons, surrounded by a dim yellow light, grabbed both my hands. They quickly put chains upon my arms and began to drag me down deeper into the heart. I screamed for Jesus, but there was no answer. I cried and fought with all my strength, but they dragged me on as if I offered no resistance at all.

As we went deeper into the heart, I felt a horrible pain as some force rubbed my body. It seemed as though my very flesh was being ripped off me. I screamed out in terror.

My captors dragged me to a cell and threw me inside. As they locked the door, I cried even louder. They laughed sarcastically and said, "It will do you no good to cry. When your time has come, you will be taken before our master. He will torment you for his pleasure."

The dreadful odor of the heart had saturated my body. "Why am I here? What is wrong? Am I crazy? Let me out! Let me out!" I cried to no avail.

After a while, I began to feel the side of the cell I was in. It was round and soft like something alive. It was alive, and it began to move. "O Lord," I screamed. "What is happening? Jesus, where are You?" But only the echo of my own voice came back in reply.

Fear—the most awesome fear—gripped my soul. For the first time since Jesus had left me, I began to realize that I was lost without any hope at all. I sobbed and called out to Jesus over and over again. Then I heard a voice in the darkness saying, "It will do you no good to call for Jesus. He is not here."

A dim light began to fill the place. For the first time, I could see other cells—cells like mine, embedded in the wall of the heart. A web of some kind was in front of us, and inside each cell a kind of muddy, gooey substance was flowing through the cells.

A woman's voice from the next cell said to me, "You are lost in this place of torment. There is no way out of here."

I could barely see her in the dimness of the light. She was awake, as I was, but the occupants of all the other cells seemed to be asleep or in a trance. "No hope," she cried, "no hope!"

A feeling of intense loneliness and utter despair fell upon me. The woman's words did not help. She said, "This is the heart of hell. Here we are tormented, but our torments are not as bad as those in other parts of hell." I found later she had lied about there not being as much torment here as there was elsewhere in hell.

"Sometimes," she continued, "we are brought before Satan and he tortures us for his pleasure. Satan feeds on our pain and grows strong on our cries of despair and sorrow. Our sins are always before us. We know we are ungodly. We know also that we once knew the Lord Jesus but refused Him and turned away from God. We did as we pleased. Before I came here I was a prostitute. I took men and women for their money and called what we did 'love.' I destroyed many homes. Many lesbians, homosexuals and adulterers are in these cells."

I cried out into the darkness, "I do not belong here. I am saved. I belong to God. Why am I here?" But there was no answer.

Then the demons came back and opened my cell door. One pulled while the other pushed me along a rough pathway. The touch of the demons was like a burning flame against my flesh. They were hurting me.

"O Jesus, where are You? Please help me, Jesus!" I cried.

A roaring fire sprang up in front of me but stopped before it touched me. Now it seemed as though my flesh was being ripped off my body. The most excruciating pain I could imagine swept over me. I was hurting beyond belief. Something unseen was tearing at my body, while evil spirits in the form of bats were biting me all over.

"Dear Lord Jesus," I cried, "Where are You? Oh, please, let me out!"

I was pushed and pulled until I came to a wide open place in the heart of hell, then I was thrown before a dirty type of altar. Upon the altar was a large, open book. I heard evil laughter and recognized I was lying in the dirt before Satan.

Satan said, "At last I have you!"

I recoiled in horror but soon realized he was not looking at me but someone in front of me. Satan said, "Ha-ha, at last I am able to destroy you from the earth. Let me see what your punishment will be." He opened the book and ran his finger down the pages. The name of the soul was called, and the punishment was meted out.

"Dear Lord," I cried, "can all this be real?"

I was next, and the demons pushed me up on a platform and forced me to bow before Satan. The same evil laughter rang out from him. "I waited for you a long time, and at last I have you," he cried with malicious delight. "You tried to escape me, but now I have you."

A fear like I had never felt before came on me. My flesh was again being torn from me, and a great chain was being wrapped around my body. I looked down at myself as the chain was placed on me. I looked like the others. I was a skeleton full of dead men's bones. Worms crawled inside of me, and a fire began at my feet and enveloped me in flames.

I cried again, "O Lord Jesus, what has happened? Where are You, Jesus?"

Satan laughed and laughed. "There is no Jesus here," he said, "I am your king now. You will be with me here forever. You are mine now."

I was gripped by the most awful emotions. I could not feel God, nor love, nor peace, nor warmth. But I could feel with the keenest of senses, fear, hatred, excruciating pain and sorrow beyond measure. I called out to the Lord Jesus to save me, but there was no answer.

Satan said, "I am your Lord now," and raised his arms to summon a demon to his side. At once, an ugly evil spirit came up on the platform where I was standing and grabbed me. He had a large body, with a face like a bat, claws for hands, and an evil odor exuded from him.

"What shall I do with her, Lord Satan?" the evil spirit asked, as another demon with hair all over his body and a face like a wild boar also grabbed me.

"Take her to the deepest part of the heart—a place where horrors are ever before her eyes. There she will learn to call me Lord."

I was dragged away to a dark, dark place and thrown into something cold and clammy. Oh, how could one feel both cold and burning at the same time? I did not know. But the fire burned my body, and the worms crawled over and through me. The moans of the dead filled the air.

"O Lord Jesus," I cried in desperation, "why am I here? Dear God, let me die."

All at once a light filled the place where I was sitting. Jesus appeared and took me into His arms, and instantly I was back in my home.

"Dear Lord Jesus, where were You?" I cried, as the tears flowed down my cheeks.

Tenderly Jesus spoke and said, "My child, hell is real. But you could never know for sure until you had experienced it for yourself. Now you know the truth and what it is really like to be lost in hell. Now you can tell others about it. I had to let you go through that so you would know without a doubt."

I was so sad and so tired. I collapsed in the arms of Jesus. And even though He restored me whole, I wanted to go far, far away—from Jesus, from my family, from everyone.

During the following days at home I was very sick. My soul was so sad, and the horrors of hell were ever before my eyes. It was many days before I was fully recovered.

11

Outer Darkness

Night after night Jesus and I went back into hell so I could record these terrible truths. Each time we passed the heart, I walked very close to Jesus. An enormous fear gripped my soul each time I remembered what happened to me there. I knew I had to go on to save souls. But it was only through the mercies of God that I could go back.

We stopped before a group of demons who were singing and chanting and praising Satan. They seemed to be enjoying themselves immensely. Jesus said, "I will let you hear what they are saying."

"We will go to this house today and torment those that are there. We will get more power from Lord Satan if we do this right," they said. "Oh, yes, we will cause a lot of pain and sickness there and much grief to them all. They began to dance and sing evil songs of worship to Satan, glorying in evil.

A demon said, "We will have to watch very carefully for those who believe in Jesus, for they can cast us out."

"Yes," said another, "at the name of Jesus we have to flee."

Then one last evil spirit said, "But we are not going to those who know Jesus and the power of His name."

"My angels," said Jesus, "keep My people from these evil spirits, and their works do not prosper. I also protect many of the unsaved, even though they do not know it. I have many angels employed to stop Satan's wicked plans."

Jesus said, "There are many demons in the air and on the earth. I have allowed you to see some of these demons, but others cannot. That is why the truth of the gospel must be preached to everyone. The truth will set men free, and I will protect them from evil. In My name there is deliverance and freedom. I have all power in heaven and earth. Do not fear Satan, but fear God."

As we walked on through hell, Jesus and I came upon a very large and very dark man. He was enshrouded in darkness and had the appearance of an angel. He was holding something in his left hand.

Jesus said, "This place is called outer darkness."

I heard weeping and gnashing of teeth. Nowhere before had there been such utter hopelessness as I felt in this place. The angel that stood before us had no wings. He looked to be about thirty feet tall, and he knew exactly what he was doing. He had a large disk in his left hand and was turning slowly with this disk lifted up high as though he was getting ready to throw it.

There was a fire in the middle of the disk, and blackness on the outer edge. The angel held his hand beneath the disk and reached far back in order to get more leverage.

I wondered who this giant angel was and what he was about to do.

Jesus knew my thoughts and said again, "This is outer darkness. Remember that my Word says, *'The children of the kingdom shall be cast out into outer darkness: there shall be weeping and gnashing of teeth.'"*

"Lord," I said, "You mean your servants are here?"

"Yes," said Jesus, "servants that turned back after I called them. Servants who loved the world more than Me and went back to wallowing in the mire of sin. Servants that would not stand for the truth and for holiness. It is better that one never starts than to turn back after beginning to serve Me."

"Believe Me," Jesus said, "if you sin, you have an advocate with the Father. If you repent of your sins, I will be faithful to cleanse you of all unrighteousness. But if you will not repent, I will come in a time you think not, and you will be cut off with the unbelievers and cast into outer darkness."

I watched the dark angel as he cast the large disk far, far out into the darkness.

"My Word means just what it says: they *'shall be cast into outer darkness.'"*

And then, immediately, Jesus and I were in the air following this disk through space. We came to the outside of the disk and stood looking in.

There was a fire in the center of the disk, and people were swimming in and out, over and under the flaming waves. There were no demons or evil spirits here, only souls burning in a sea of fire.

Outside the disk was the blackest of darkness. Only the light from the flames in the disk illuminated the night air. In that light I saw people trying to swim to the edges of the disk. Some of them would almost reach the sides when a suction force from inside the disk would drag them back into the flames. I watched as their forms turned to skeletons with misty-gray souls. I knew then that this was just another part of hell.

And then I saw, as in a vision, angels opening seals. Nations and kingdoms appeared to be locked beneath them. As the angels broke the seals, men and women, boys and girls marched straight into the flames.

I watched in ghastly fascination, wondering if I knew any of the fallen servants of the Lord who were marching past. I could not turn my head away from the sight of souls marching into the fire, and no one was trying to stop them.

I cried, "Lord, please stop them before they reach the fire!"

But Jesus said, "He who has ears should hear. He who has eyes should see. My child, cry out against sin and evil. Tell my servants to be faithful and to call upon the name of the Lord. I am taking you through this awful place so that you can tell them about hell."

Jesus continued, "Some will not believe you. Some will say God is too good to send men and women to hell. But tell them My Word is true. Tell them that the fearful and unbelieving will have their part in the lake of fire."

12

Horns

J esus said, "Tonight, My child, we will go to different part of the heart of hell. I want to tell you about the horns and show you how they will be used to funnel evil spirits and demon forces up to the surface of the earth."

As Jesus spoke, I began to witness an open vision. In the vision, I saw an old farmhouse, dead and gray-looking, surrounded with many dead trees and high, dead grass. The yard around the farmhouse was littered with dead things. There was no life there. The farmhouse looked as though it had settled at the corners and was sinking into the center of the field. There were no other buildings in sight.

Death was everywhere. I knew this farmhouse was part of hell, but I could not yet understand what I was seeing. Inside, behind the dingy windows, loomed large shadows in human shapes. There was something evil about their appearance. One of the shapes moved toward the front door and opened it.

I watched as a huge man with extremely large muscles came out of the door and walked onto the porch. I saw him clearly. He was about six feet tall, with the bulky build of a weight lifter. His color was the same dead gray as the surroundings. He wore only a pair of men's pants. They were as gray and dead-looking as the bare skin of his upper body. His flesh was like scales, and his head was very big. In fact, his head was so large that his legs were bowed from carrying such a great load. His feet were hoofed like the feet of a pig. His face was stern and evil, and he looked to be very old. His eyes were dead, and his face was very broad.

In the vision, I saw this awful creature walk off the old porch. The earth shook as he moved, and horns were growing out of the top of his head—large horns that grew up, up and out of sight. As he walked, I saw that the horns were growing, ever so slowly. Other horns also began to grow from his head. Little horns sprang from the bigger ones. I saw that his head was like a beast—a powerful evil beast, full of destruction. Each step he took shook the earth.

Jesus said, "Watch."

I saw the horns as they wound their way upward and ended in homes, churches, hospitals, offices and buildings of all kinds all over the earth. The horns did great damage throughout the land. I saw the beast speak and evil spirits were spit out on the earth. I saw many people seduced by these demonic forces and fall into Satan's snares.

We are in a war—good against evil, I thought.

"We are in a war," I heard the Spirit of the Lord say. "Good against evil."

Dark clouds came out of the horns and hid the many forms of evil that were going out upon the earth. All the abominations that God hates were there. I saw kingdoms arising out of the earth, and millions of people began to follow these evil forces. I saw the old horns removed and new ones grow in their places.

I heard Jesus say, "This is beginning to happen now! These things are, and were, and will be. Men will become lovers of themselves instead of God. Evil will be rampant in the last days. Men and women will love their homes, cars, lands, buildings, businesses, their silver and their gold more than Me.

"**Repent,**" He said, "for I am a jealous God. Nothing can be placed before your worship of Me —not sons or daughters or wives or husbands. For God is a Spirit, and He must be worshiped in Spirit and truth."

I watched as the horns moved over the face of the earth, rising high into the heavens. New kingdoms arose, and there was war and destruction throughout the land. They that worshiped the beast were many.

The evil beast with the horns walked back and forth as if thinking, and the earth shook under his weight. After some minutes he returned to the farmhouse. Dark clouds arose, and many were dead in the land.

I saw the world in the midst of a great tribulation, and I began praying with all my heart. "O Lord, help us," I cried out. Then two large beasts in spirit forms rose out of the earth and began to make war with each other. I knew they came from hell.

A sea of people stood watching the fight between these two evils. And then I saw something rise from the ground between them. They stopped fighting and stood on each side of a big ship. Both beasts tried to destroy the ship, but they could not. They pushed it back beneath the earth, and buried it between the two of them. They stood face to face again, ready to resume their warfare.

I heard a voice say, "Watch."

As I watched, a light appeared on the ground where the ship was buried. The ship then reappeared on the surface of the ground and became a large disk. The two beasts began to take on other forms and became large and black. A door in front of the disk opened, and a strong beam of light revealed a flight of stairs. The stairs went down, down into the earth, and I heard a voice say, "Into hell!"

There was a strong sense of evil in the air, and I felt lost and undone as I watched. A paralyzing force came out of the disk, and I had nowhere to run. I felt trapped, even though I was in the Spirit.

Almost at once, Jesus lifted me up higher and higher until I was looking down on the vision. But now the stairs had become an escalator, which was moving up and down from the heart of the earth.

When I was beside Jesus, I felt safe and protected. "It shall come out of hell," I heard a voice say.

Jesus said, "This shall be. This is yet to come. Write for all to know."

In my vision the escalator was bringing up demon forces and evil spirits. The two beasts stood, one on each side of the ship, and I saw them begin to change again. I heard the sound of a great roar—the sound of motors running at a high rate of speed. The beasts' heads got large, and a light began to fill their hands. I saw the two beasts and the ship as the three of them were joined together.

Many souls, as if walking in their sleep, marched into one of the beasts. For hours I watched this gruesome sight, until at last, one of the beasts was packed with people. As I listened, from the first beast came a great roar as if a plane was getting ready for takeoff. The beast had gotten his power from the ship. As he began to fly, he was again in the form of a man. As he flew, his head seemed to be full of lights and great powers emanated from him.

As he disappeared into the heavens, his head became the ship again.

I could still hear the sound of the first beast as I watched the second beast fill up with souls. When he was full, I saw the second beast begin to go straight up like a rocket. He joined the other beast, and they both moved slowly away into the gray sky. The second beast had also taken on the form of a man. I heard their loud roar as they went out of sight.

I wondered what this meant. I saw the ship, or disk, settle itself back into the earth. The earth closed up over it until it was again out of sight. As the vision began to fade, I saw a large courtroom, and I thought of the great white throne judgment.

13

The Right Arm of Hell

After the first vision, Jesus and I went to a different part of hell. Jesus said, "These things you are seeing are for the end times." Another vision appeared before me.

Jesus said, "We are in the right arm of hell."

We walked up a high, dry hill. At the top of the hill, I looked below and saw a swirling river. There were no pits of fire or demons or evil spirits, only the large river flowing between unseen banks. The banks of the river were hidden in the darkness. Jesus and I walked closer to the river, and I saw that it was full of blood and fire.

As I looked closer, I saw many souls, each chained to another. The weight of the chains dragged them under the surface of the lake of fire.

The souls in hell were in the fire of hell. I saw also that they were in the form of skeletons with misty-gray souls.

"What is this?" I asked the Lord.

"These are the souls of the unbelievers and the ungodly. These were lovers of their own flesh more than lovers of God. They were men loving men, and women loving women, who would not repent and be saved from their sin. They enjoyed their life of sin and spurned My salvation."

I stood beside Jesus and looked into the lake of fire. The fire began to roar like a great furnace, moving and devouring everything in its path. Soon it filled nearly the entire right arm of hell.

The fire approached to within feet of us, but did not touch us. The river was burning everything in its path. I watched Jesus' face, and it was sad and tender. He still had love and compassion for these lost souls written on His countenance. I began to cry and wished I could leave this place of torment, to go on was almost unbearable.

I looked again at the souls in the fire. They were a fiery red, and their bones were blackened and burned. I heard their souls cry out in regret and sorrow.

The Lord said, "This is their torment. Chain after chain, they are linked together. These desired the flesh of their own kind, men with men, and women with women, doing that which is unnatural. They led many young girls and young boys into acts of sin. They called it love, but in the end it was sin and death.

"I know that many boys and girls, men and women were forced against their wills to commit such atrocious acts—I know and will not hold this sin to their charge. Remember this though," said Jesus, "I know all things, and the persons who made these youths to sin have the greater punishment. I will judge righteously. To the sinner, I say, 'Repent, and I will have mercy. Call on Me and I will hear.'

"Time after time I called to these souls to repent and to come unto Me. I would have forgiven them and cleansed them; and in My name they could have been set free. But they would not listen to Me. They wanted the lust of the flesh more than the love of the living God. Because I am holy, you must be holy. Touch not the unclean thing, and I will receive you," said the Lord.

I felt very sick as I looked at the souls in the lake of fire.

"If only they had turned to Me before it was too late," Jesus continued. "My blood was shed so that everyone could come to Me. I gave My life that even the vilest of sinners might live."

Multitudes of souls went by in the river of flames. Over and under the waves of fire, they went with no way out of the burning and swimming in the lake of fire. I heard cries of regret as the bloody river flowed by us.

We walked up a trail beside the river. In front of us, sitting on a hill, was a large woman. She swayed back and forth as though she was drunk. Written on her were the words *"Mystery Babylon."*

I now knew the mother of abominations on the earth came from hell. An evil, powerful force emanated from her. I saw multitudes, peoples and tongues beneath her. She had seven heads and ten horns. In her was found the blood of the prophets, the saints and all that were slain upon the earth.

"Come out from her and be separate", said the Lord. "In her time she shall be destroyed."

We walked on past the evil woman with the horns on her head. Everything began to get dark. Now Jesus was the only light. We walked until we came to another hillside. In the distance I could see hot flames in the air. The atmosphere became oppressively hot.

We went around the hill and came to a large door with slots cut in it. It was set into the side of the hill. A large chain was on the door, and flames raged from it. The door was also bolted with large locks. I wondered what it all meant.

All at once, the dark figure of a man, attired in a long, dark cape, appeared in front of the door. His face looked to be very old and very tired. The skin of his face was pulled tightly against the bones of his skull. He looked to be a thousand years old.

Jesus said to me, "Behind that doorway is the bottomless pit. My Word is true."

The flames behind the door reached higher until the door bulged from the pressure of the heat.

"Dear Lord," I said, "I'll be glad when Satan is cast into the bottomless pit and all these evil things stop for a season."

He replied, "Come, hear what the Spirit is saying to the churches. The end is near, and I am calling sinners to repent and be saved. Look now."

We were standing in a clearing, and I was with the Lord in the Spirit. I looked and beheld an open vision. In the vision I saw a fiery serpent begin to strike the air with his enormous tail. I watched as this spiritual serpent moved with awesome power.

Then I saw him go back into the right arm of hell and wait. I knew that He could not strike the earth until God's Word would be fulfilled.

I saw fire and smoke ascend out of the earth, and I saw a strange mist as it formed over the earth. I saw patches of darkness appear here and there. Horns began to grow on the head of the fiery serpent. They spread out until they covered the whole earth. Satan gave orders to the fiery serpent. There were evil spirits and devils present. Then I saw the evil, fiery serpent come out of the right arm of hell and begin to strike the earth with great force, hurting and destroying many people.

Jesus said, "This will happen in the end times. Come up higher."

Reader, if you are committing any of the sins I have written about, please stop sinning and call upon Jesus to save you. You do not have to go to hell. Call upon the Lord while He is near. He will hear you and save you. Whoever calls on the name of the Lord will be saved.

14

The Left Arm of Hell

A Prophecy From Jesus to All

Jesus said, "These things are now beginning in the earth, are yet to be, and are soon coming upon all the earth. The fiery serpent is part of the beast. These prophecies you are about to read are true. The revelations are true. Watch and pray. Love one another. Keep yourselves holy. Keep your hands clean.

"Husbands, love your wives as Christ loved the church. Husbands and wives, love each other as I have loved you. I ordained marriage and blessed it with My Word. Keep the marriage bed holy. Cleanse yourself from all unrighteousness and be pure, even as I am pure.

"The holy people of God have been led away by flatterers. Do not be deceived; God is not mocked. Understanding will come to you if you will open your ears and listen to Me. This is the Lord's message to the churches. Beware of false prophets who stand in My holy place and deceive with flatteries. O earth, My holy people have fallen asleep to the sound of false doctrine. Awake, Awake! I tell you that all unrighteousness is sin. Cleanse yourself from all sin of the flesh and the spirit.

"My holy prophets lived holy lives, but you have rebelled against Me and My holiness. You have brought evil upon yourself. You have sinned and brought yourself into bondage to sickness and death. You have committed iniquity and have done wickedly and have rebelled against Me. You have departed from My precepts and from My judgments. You have not hearkened to the words of My servants, the prophet and the prophetess. Curses instead of blessings have come upon you, and still you refuse to return to me and repent of your sins.

"If you will return and repent and if you will honor Me with the fruit of righteousness, I will bless your homes and honor your marriage beds. If you will humble yourselves and call upon Me, I will hear you and bless you.

"Listen, you ministers of My Holy Word. Do not teach My people to sin against their God. Remember that judgment begins at the house of God; unless you repent, I will remove you for the sins you have taught My people. Do you think that I am blind that I cannot see and deaf that I cannot hear?

"You who hold the truth in unrighteousness and line your pockets with silver and gold at the expense of the poor—repent, I say, before it is too late. On the day of judgment you will stand alone before Me to give an account of what you did with My Holy Word. If you call upon Me in repentance, I will remove the curse from your lands and bless you with a mighty blessing. If you will repent and be ashamed of your sins, I will have mercy and compassion on you, and I will not remember your sins anymore. Pray that you may be an overcomer.

"Awake to life and live. Repent to the people you have led astray and taught false doctrine. Tell them you have sinned and that you have scattered My sheep. Repent to them.

"Behold, I am preparing a holy army. They will do mighty exploits for me and destroy your high places. They are an army of holy men and women, boys and girls. They have been anointed to preach the true gospel, to lay hands on the sick and to call the sinner to repentance.

"This is an army of working men, housewives, single men, single women and school children. They are common people, for not many noble have responded to My call. In the past they have been misunderstood and mistreated, abused and rejected. But I have blessed them with boldness in holiness and in spirit. They will begin to fulfill My prophecy and to do My will. I will walk in them, talk in them and work in them.

"These are they who have turned to me with all their heart, soul, mind and strength. This army will awaken many to righteousness and purity of spirit. I will soon begin to move upon them, to choose for My army those I desire. I will search for them in the cities and in the towns. Many will be surprised at those I have chosen. You will see them begin to move across the land and do exploits for My name's sake. Watch and see My power at work.

"Again I tell you, do not defile the marriage bed. Do not defile the body in which the Holy Ghost dwells. Sins of the body lead to sins of the spirit. Keep the marriage bed holy. I made man for woman and woman for man and decreed that the two should be united in holy matrimony. Again, I say awake."

———————————

I saw many other visions in the left arm of hell. I was instructed by the Lord that I must not reveal them now. Many of them were visions of the world in the end-times, when many of the people of God will fall away and be lost.

In the visions, I was given revelations about the body of Christ, the ministry of the sons of God, the children of the beast and the ultimate return of Christ. "Later, you may reveal them," He said, "but not now."

"This army," said the Lord, "which was spoken of by the prophet Joel, will arise from the land and do great works for God. The Son of Righteousness shall arise with healing in His wings. He shall tread down the wicked, and they shall be ashes under the soles of His feet.

"They shall be called the army of the Lord. I will give gifts unto them, and they will accomplish My mighty works. They shall do exploits for the

Lord of glory. I will pour out My Spirit upon all flesh, and your sons and daughters shall prophesy.

"This army shall fight against the forces of evil and shall destroy much of Satan's work. They shall win many to Jesus Christ before the day the evil beast arises," said the Lord.

Jesus said, "Come, it is time to go now."

At last we were leaving the visions and the left arm of hell. I was very glad.

As we departed, Jesus said, "Tell your families I love them and correct them in love. Tell them that I will keep them from evil if they will put their trust in Me."

15

The Days of Joel

I heard a voice say, "Write, for these things are faithful and true." Again, I was with the Lord in the Spirit. He was high and lifted up, and His voice was like thunder.

"Behold, O earth, these things are, were and are to come. I am the First and the Last. Serve Me, the Creator, for I give life, not death. Arise from your evil and call upon Me, and I will heal and deliver you. The things you read in this book are true, and they will soon come to pass.

"Repent, for the time is at hand, and the Lord of glory will soon appear. Be ready, for you do not know the day nor the hour. Great shall be the reward of those who await My coming. I will bless My little ones, those that have kept the faith and have served Me in truth and righteousness. Before they know it, it will be upon them. I have prepared a blessing for those who have been faithful to their calling and those that have not denied My name.

"I say, if My people, who are called by My name, will humble themselves and pray, I will forgive them and heal them and restore their losses. I desire to hear, to deliver, and to save all who believe and call upon My name.

"Sanctify a fast. Call a solemn assembly. Gather the elders and all the inhabitants of the lands into My house, and cry unto Me. Alas, for the day of the Lord comes as a thief in the night—the day is at hand.

"Trust Me, and I will restore unto you the years the locusts, the cankerworm, the caterpillar and the palmer worm have eaten.

"My great army which I have called will not break their ranks nor their stride. They will do marvelous exploits, and they shall not be conquered, for I am their strength. Their voices will sound like the trumpet, like the thunders will they sound, and all will hear and know that I am the Lord your God."

*   *   *

Dear Lord Jesus, it is my prayer that I be counted worthy to be in this army. I want to be in this army, but I know I must be pure and holy as Jesus is pure and holy. By the blood Jesus shed, cleanse me from all unrighteousness. Help me to keep a repentant heart, free of all hatred and bitterness.

Father, I know that many of Your people are asleep. I fear You will have to break our vessels of clay and humble us if there are to be fruits of righteousness.

Lord, I do not want to go to hell again and have to stay there. O Lord, help me to warn the people. Give me power to stop hell from enlarging itself. Help me and Your people to be good, kindhearted, forgiving and loving to one another. Help us to speak the truth at all times.

I know that Jesus Christ is returning soon, and His rewards are with Him. I know that my message to the world is "Repent, for the day of the Lord is at hand." Father, I do not want the blood of this people on my hands.

16

The Center of Hell

Again the Lord and I went into hell. Jesus said to me, "My child, for this purpose you were born, to write and tell what I have told you and shown you. For these things are faithful and true. I have called you forth to tell the world through you that there is a hell, but I have made a way of escape. I will not show you all parts of hell. And there are hidden things which I cannot reveal to you. But I will show you much. Now come and see the powers of darkness and their end."

We went again to the belly of hell and began to walk toward a small opening. I turned to look where we were entering and found that we were on a ledge beside a cell in the center of hell. We stopped in front of a cell in which was a beautiful woman. Over the top of the cell were the letters "B.C."

I heard the woman say, "Lord, I knew you would come someday. Please let me out of this place of torment." She was dressed in the clothes of an ancient era, and she was very beautiful. I knew that she had been here for many centuries but could not die. Her soul was in torment. She began to pull at the bars and cry.

Softly Jesus said, "Peace, be still." He spoke to her with sadness in His voice. "Woman, you know why you are here."

"Yes," she said, "but I can change. I remember when You let all those others out of paradise. I remember Your words of salvation. I will be good now," she cried, "and I will serve You." She clenched the bars of the cell in her tiny fists and began to scream, "Let me out! Let me out!"

At that, she began to change before our eyes. Her clothing began to burn. Her flesh fell off, and all that remained was a black skeleton with burned-out holes for eyes and a hollow shell of a soul. I watched in horror as the old woman fell to the floor. All her beauty had departed in a moment. It staggered my imagination to think that she had been here since before Christ was born.

Jesus said to her, "You knew on earth what your end would be. Moses gave you the law, and you heard it. But instead of obeying My law, you chose to be an instrument in the hands of Satan, a soothsayer and witch. You even taught the art of witchcraft. You loved darkness rather than light, and your deeds were evil. If you had repented with your heart, My Father would have forgiven you. But now, it is too late."

With sorrow and great pity in our hearts, we walked away. There would never be an end to her pain and sufferings. Her bony hands reached out to us as we walked on.

"My child," said the Lord, "Satan uses many devices to destroy good men and women. He works day and night, trying to get people to serve him. If you fail to choose to serve God, you have chosen to serve the devil. Choose life, and the truth will set you free."

After walking for a short distance, we stopped in front of another cell. I heard a man's voice calling out, "Who is there? Who is there?" I wondered why he called out.

Jesus said, "He is blind."

I heard a sound and looked about. Ahead of us was a large demon with huge wings which appeared to be broken. He looked right past us. I stood close to Jesus.

Together, we turned to look at the man who had spoken. He also was in a cell, and his back was to us—he was a skeleton form with fire and the smell of death on him. He was flailing the air and crying out, "Help me. Help, someone!"

Tenderly, Jesus said, "Man, peace, be still."

The man turned and said, "Lord, I knew You would come for me. I repent now. Please let me out. I know I was a horrible person and used my handicap for selfish gain. I know I was a sorcerer and deceived many for Satan. But Lord, I repent now. Please let me out. Day and night I am tormented in these flames, there is no water. I am so thirsty." He cried, "won't You give me a drink of water?"

The man was still calling after Jesus as we walked away. I looked down in sadness.

Jesus said, "All sorcerers and workers of evil will have their part in the lake which burns with fire and brimstone, which is the second death."

We came to another cell in which was another man. He said, "Lord, I knew You would come and release me. I have repented for a long time." This man also was a skeleton, full of flames and worms.

"O man, you are still full of lies and sin. You know you were a disciple of Satan, a liar who deceived many. The truth was never in your mouth, and death was always your reward. You heard My words often and made fun of My salvation and My Holy Spirit. You lied all your life and would not listen to Me. You are of your father the devil. All liars will have their part in the lake of fire. You have blasphemed the Holy Ghost."

The man began to curse and say many evil things against the Lord. We went on. This soul was forever lost in hell.

Jesus said, "Whoever will may come to Me, and he that loses his life for My sake shall find life, and that more abundantly. But sinners must repent while still alive on earth. It is too late to repent when they arrive here. Many sinners want to serve God and Satan, or they believe that they have unlimited time to accept the grace God offers. The truly wise will choose this day whom they will serve."

Soon we came to the next cell. A desperate cry of sorrow came from within. We looked and saw a skeleton of a man huddled on a floor. His bones were black from burning, and his soul was a dirty-gray mist inside. I noticed that parts of his body were missing. Smoke and flames came up around him. Worms crawled inside of him.

Jesus said, "This man's sins were many. He was a murderer and had hate in his heart. He would not repent or even believe that I would forgive him. If he had only come to Me!"

"You mean, Lord," I asked, "he thought that You would not forgive him of murder and hatred?"

"Yes," said Jesus. "If only he had believed and come to Me, I would have forgiven him all his sins, great and small. Instead, he continued to sin and died in them. That is why he is where he is today. He was given many opportunities to serve Me and to believe the gospel, but he refused. Now it is too late."

The next cell we came to was filled with a terrible odor. I could hear the cries of the dead and moans of regret everywhere. I felt so sad that I was almost sick. I made up my mind that I would do all I could to tell the world about this place.

A woman's voice said, "Help me." I stared into a real pair of eyes, not the burned-out sockets which were the marks of burning. I was so sad I shivered, and I felt such pity and sorrow for this soul. I wanted so badly to pull her out of the cell and run away with her. "It's so painful," she said.

"Lord, I will do what is right now. I once knew You, and You were my Savior." Her hands clenched the bars of the cell. "Why won't you be my Savior now?" Big pieces of burning flesh fell from her, and only bones clenched the bars.

"You even healed me of cancer," she said. "You told me to go and sin no more lest a worse thing come upon me. I tried, Lord; You know I tried. I even tried to witness for You. But, Lord, I soon learned that those who preach Your Word are not popular. I wanted people to like me. I slowly went back into the world and the lust of the flesh devoured me. Nightclubs and strong drink became more important than You. I lost touch with my Christian friends and soon found myself seven times worse than I had been before.

"And though I became lovers of both men and women, I never intended to be lost. I did not know that I was possessed by Satan. I still felt Your call upon my heart to repent and be saved, but I would not. I kept thinking I still had time. Tomorrow I will turn back to Jesus, and He will forgive me and deliver me. But I waited too long, and now it is too late," she cried.

Her sad eyes burst into flames and disappeared. I screamed and fell against Jesus. O Lord, I thought, how easily could that have been me or one of my loved ones! Please, sinner, wake up before it is too late.

We walked on to another cell. In it another man with a skeleton form and a dirty-gray soul inside. Cries of such utter pain and regret came from this man that I knew I could never forget them.

Jesus said, "My child, some who read this book will compare it to a fiction story or a movie they have seen. They will say this is not true. But you know these things are true. You know that hell is real, for I have brought you here many times by My Spirit. I have revealed the truth to you so that you can witness to it."

Lost person, if you will not repent and be baptized and believe the gospel of Jesus Christ, this will surely be your end.

"This man is here," said the Lord, "because of his rebellion. The sin of rebellion is like the sin of witchcraft. In fact, all those who know My Word and My ways and have heard the gospel but still will not repent are in rebellion against Me. Many are in hell today because of this sin."

The man spoke to Jesus and said, "I once thought about making You Lord of my life, but I did not want to walk Your straight and narrow way. I wanted the broad way. It was so much easier to serve sin. I did not want to have to be righteous. I loved my sinful way. I desired to drink strong drink and do the things of this world more than obey Your commands. But I wish now I had listened to those You sent to me. Instead, I did evil and would not repent."

Great sobs shook his body as he cried out in regret. "For years I have been tormented in this place. I know what I am, and I know I will never get out. I am tormented day and night in these flames and these worms. I cry, but no one comes to help. No one cares for my soul here—no one cares for my soul." He fell into a small heap on the floor and continued to cry.

We walked on to another cell. A woman sat picking the worms off her bones. She began to cry when she saw Jesus. "Help me, Lord," she said, "I will be good. Please let me out." She also arose and clenched the bars of the cell. I felt such great pity for her. As she cried, sobs shook her body.

She said, "Lord, when I was on earth, I worshiped the Hindu gods and many idols. I would not believe the gospel the missionaries preached to me, although I heard it many times. One day I died. I cried for my gods to save me from hell, but they could not. Now, Lord, I'd like to repent."

"It's too late," said Jesus.

Flames covered her form as we walked on; her cries still fill my soul even now. Satan had deceived her.

With sadness in His voice Jesus said, "Come, we will return tomorrow. It is time to go now."

17

War in the Heavens

The Spirit of the Lord was upon me, and again we went into hell. Jesus said, "I tell you the truth, many souls are here because of witchcraft, the occult, the worship of other gods, disobedience, unbelief, drunkenness, and filthiness of flesh and spirit. Come, I will show you a mystery and tell you of hidden things. I will reveal to you how to pray against the forces of evil."

We walked into a part of hell next to the evil heart. Jesus said, "We are soon going into the jaws of hell, but I desire to reveal to all that hell has enlarged itself."

We stopped, and he said, "Behold and believe." I looked and beheld an open vision. In the vision, Jesus and I were high above the earth looking out into space. I saw a spiritual circle high above the earth. The circle was invisible to the natural eye, but in the spirit, I could see it well. I knew that the vision was related to our fight against the princes and powers of the air.

As I continued to look, I discovered there were, in fact, several circles. In the first circle were many dirty, evil spirits. I saw the dirty spirits take on the forms of witches, and they began to fly about the heavens and do much spiritual damage. I heard the voice of Jesus say, "In My name, I give My children power over these evil ones. Listen and learn how to pray."

I saw an odd-shaped form arise from another circle and begin to spin about and cast spells. I saw then that a demon had arisen, and he was doing evil things to the earth. The demon had the spirit of a wizard. He would turn and laugh, and from a stick in his hand, he cast evil spells on various people. I saw other evil spirits join the wizard, and Satan gave him more power.

"Behold, what you bind on earth, I will bind in heaven," said Jesus. "Satan must be bound if the prayers of the saints are to be effective in these last days."

From another circle, I saw another sorcerer arise, and he began to give orders. Rain and fire fell upon the earth as he spoke. He spoke many evil things, and he deceived the people on the earth. As I watched, I saw two more evil spirits join the sorcerer high above the earth. These all were evil princes and powers of the air.

These gave their powers to witches who were gathered together in a certain place to do evil. Workers of darkness gathered around them. The spirits came and went as they chose.

"Watch carefully," Jesus said, "for the Holy Spirit is revealing a great truth to you."

In the vision I saw terrible things happening on the earth. Evil was magnified and sin abounded. The forces of evil caused men to steal, to lie, to cheat, to hurt one another, to speak evil and to succumb to the lusts of the flesh. All kinds of evil were released upon the earth.

I said, "Jesus, this is awful to behold."

Jesus said, "My child, in My name, evil has to flee. Put on the whole armor of God that you may be able to stand in the evil day, and having done all, to stand."

As the evil spirits spewed their vileness and slander upon the earth, I saw the people of God begin to pray. They prayed in the name of Jesus and in faith. As they prayed, the Word of God came against the evil spirits, which began to lose ground. As the saints prayed, the forces of evil lost their hold. Evil spells were broken. Those who had been weakened by the forces of hell were strengthened.

When they prayed as in one voice, the angels of heaven entered the fray. I saw the holy angels fighting with the evil princes and powers of the air, and God's angels were destroying the powers of evil.

I looked, and behold there were rows upon rows of angel forces, with about 600 in each row. As the people believed God, the angels advanced. God gave the orders, and mighty was His power. He gave great strength to His people and to the angels to destroy the works of Satan. God was fighting against evil in the sky.

When the people prayed and believed God, the evil forces were destroyed. But when there was disbelief, the evil powers began to overcome.

"My people must believe, and they must agree with each other and with Me," said the Lord, "if all things are to be put under the Father's feet." Heaven and earth must agree if we are to destroy our enemies.

As the praises of God's people began to rise from the earth, the evil forces retreated. I saw saints of God praying with all their hearts against the wiles of the devil. As they did, evil spells and curses were broken, and the saints gained the victory.

This is what happened. As the angels of the Lord fought with the demons and the forces of hell, saints were delivered through prayer. As the people were delivered, many praises rang out to God, and the praises brought more victories. Only when the results of prayer were not seen at once did the praises cease and evil began to win the battle.

I heard an angel with a loud voice say, "O Lord, the faith of Your people is weak. They must have faith if You are to deliver them from the hordes of Satan. Lord, have mercy on the heirs of salvation."

The voice of the Almighty responded, "Without faith it is impossible to please God. But the Lord is faithful, and He will establish you."

Again in the vision I saw God pour out His Spirit on all flesh, and the people believed that God would do all they asked because they were His and sincerely loved Him. They had faith in God and believed His Word, and God delivered them. And the Word of God grew in the land.

The Lord said, "All things are possible to them that believe. I watch over My Word to perform it. You do your part, and you can know that I will do Mine. If my people will stand for truth and fight the good fight, wonderful things will happen as on the Day of Pentecost. Call upon Me and I will hear. I will be your God and you will be My people. I will establish you in righteousness, truth and sincerity."

In the vision, I saw Christians being born as little babies. I saw the angels standing over them to protect them from harm. I saw the Lord of Hosts fighting their battles and gaining the victory for them. Then I saw the babes grow up and harvest the fields of the Lord of Glory. They were doing the work of the Lord with a glad heart—loving God, trusting God and serving God. I saw the angels and God's Word combine to destroy evil from the face of the earth. I saw peace on earth as everything was eventually put under the feet of God.

18

Open Visions from Hell

The Lord said, "This vision is for the future, and it will come to pass. But I shall return to redeem My bride, My church, and they shall not see it. Awaken, O My people! Sound the alarm to the corners of the earth, for I shall return as My Word has spoken."

I beheld the fiery serpent that was in the right arm of hell.

Jesus said, "Come, see what the Spirit is saying to the world."

I saw the horns of the fiery serpent as they entered the bodies of people on earth. Many were completely possessed by the serpent. As I watched, I saw a huge beast arise in a large place and turn into a man. The inhabitants of the earth ran from him, some into the wilderness, some into caves, and some into subway stations and bomb shelters. They sought any shelter to hide from the eyes of the beast. No one was praising God or talking about Jesus.

A voice said to me, "Where are My people?"

I looked closer and saw people like dead men walking. There was a desperate sadness in the air, and no one turned to the right or left. I saw that the people were being led about by some unseen force. Now and then a voice spoke to them out of the air, and they obeyed the voice. They did not talk to one another. I saw too that the number *"666"* was written on each one's forehead and on his hands. I saw soldiers on horses herding the people about as though they were cattle.

The American flag, tattered and torn, lay forlornly on the ground. There was no joy, no laughter, no happiness. I saw death and evil everywhere.

The people walked one behind another into a large department store. They kept in step like discouraged soldiers and were dressed identically in a type of prison garb. A fence surrounded the store, and guards were stationed here and there. Everywhere I looked, I saw soldiers in battle-dress uniforms.

I saw these zombie-like people herded into the store, where they were able to buy only the barest necessities. As each completed his purchases, he was placed aboard a large green army truck. The truck, well-guarded, was then driven to another area.

Here, in a type of clinic, these people were examined for communicable diseases or crippling handicaps. A small number of them were shuffled to the side as rejects.

Soon, those who failed the examination were taken to another room. In that room, an impressive array of switches, buttons and gauges lined an entire wall. A door opened, and several technicians came in. One of them began to call the names of the people in the room. Without a struggle, they arose when their names were called and marched into a large box. When they were inside, another technician closed the door and pulled a switch in a panel on the wall.

A few minutes later he opened the door, took down a broom and dust pan, and swept what remained of them off the floor. Nothing but a bit of dust was left of what had once been a roomful of people!

I saw those people who passed the medical exam being put back into the same truck and driven to a train. No one spoke or even turned to look at anyone else. At another building each person was assigned a job. They all went to work without a single dispute. I watched as they worked very hard at their assigned tasks, and then at the end of the day, they were taken to an apartment building with a high fence around it. Each undressed and went to bed. Tomorrow they would work hard again.

I heard a loud voice fill the night air.

I saw a huge beast, and he sat on a large throne. All the people obeyed the beast. I saw spiritual horns growing from his head. They reached into and out of every place on earth. The beast took upon himself many positions of authority and many offices, and he became great in power.

The beast pushed himself into many places and deceived many people. The rich and the famous were deceived as well as the poor and disfranchised. Small and great paid homage to the beast.

A large machine was brought into an office. The beast put his mark on it, and his voice came out of it. There was also a "big brother" machine that could see into homes and businesses. Only a single machine of this type existed, and it belonged to the beast. The part of the machine that was located in the homes of the people was invisible to the naked eye, but it could and did report to the beast every move the people made. I watched as the beast turned his throne around and faced toward me. On his forehead was the number *666*.

As I watched, I saw another man in another office become very angry at the beast. He demanded to talk with him. He was yelling at the top of his voice. The beast appeared and seemed very courteous as he said, "Come, I can help you take care of all your problems."

The beast took the angry man into a large room and motioned for him to lie down on a table. The room and the table reminded me of a hospital emergency room. The man was given an anesthesia and wheeled beneath a vast machine. The beast attached wires to the man's head and turned on the machine. On the top of the machine were the words, "This mind eraser belongs to the beast, 666."

When the man was removed from the table, his eyes had a vacant stare, and his movements reminded one of a zombie in a movie. I saw a large blank spot on the top of his head, and I knew his mind had been surgically altered so he could be controlled by the beast.

The beast said, "Now, sir, don't you feel better? Didn't I say I could take care of all your problems? I have given you a new mind. You will have no worries or troubles now."

The man did not speak.

"You will obey my every command," said the beast as he picked up a small object and attached it to the man's shirt. He spoke again to the man, and he answered without moving his lips. He moved like a living dead man.

"You will work and not get angry or frustrated, nor will you cry or be sad. You will work for me until you die. I have many like you that I control. Some lie, some kill, some steal, some make war, some have children, some run machinery, and some do other things. Yes, I control everything." An evil laugh came from him.

The man was handed papers to sign. He gladly gave all his belongings to the beast.

In my vision I saw the man leave the office of the beast, get in a car and drive home. When he approached his wife, she tried to kiss him, but he made no attempt to respond. He had no feeling for his wife or anyone else. The beast had made him incapable of feeling any emotion.

The wife became very angry and screamed at her husband, but to no avail. At last she said, "OK, I'll call the beast. He will know what to do." After a quick phone call, she left the house and drove to the same building her husband had just left.

The beast welcomed her in and said, "Tell me all your troubles. I am sure I can help you."

A very handsome man took her by the arm and led her to the same table her husband had been on earlier. After the same operation, she also became a depersonalized slave of the beast.

I heard the beast ask her, "How do you feel?" She did not answer until after he had attached a small object to her blouse. Then she acknowledged that he was master and lord and began to worship him.

"You will be a breeder," he said. "You will have perfect babies, and they will worship and serve me."

The woman replied in a robotic voice, "Yes, master, I will obey."

I saw the woman again. This time she was in another building. There were many pregnant women there. The women lay lifelessly on their beds and in chanted monotones praised the beast. All had *666* on their foreheads.

When their babies were born, they were taken to another building where mind-altered nurses had the task of raising them. The nurses also had *666* on their foreheads.

The beast grew in power until his empire stretched across the earth. The babies also grew, and at a certain time, they also went beneath the mind-destroying machine. They worshiped the beast and his image. But the machine had no power over the children of God.

I heard the voice of the Lord say, "Those that worship the beast and his image shall perish. Many shall be deceived and will fall, but I will save my children from the beast. These things will take place in the end times. Do not take the mark of the beast. Repent now before it is too late.

"The beast will call himself a man of peace. And he will bring peace to many nations out of a very chaotic time. He will be able to supply the world with many inexpensive goods, and he will assure that everyone's pay is sufficient. He will make an alliance with many nations, and the great men of the world will follow him into a false sense of security.

"Before these times I will raise up an army of believers that will stand for truth and righteousness. The mighty army that Joel spoke about will hear My voice from the rising to the going down of the sun.

"In the night hours also they will hear My voice, and they will answer Me. They will work for Me, and they will run like mighty men of war. They shall do great works for Me, for I will be with them."

All these things were revealed to me by the Lord Jesus Christ in an open vision. They are the words of His mouth, and they concern the times of the end.

Jesus and I returned home, and I wondered about all the things He had shown me and told me. I fell asleep praying for the salvation of all mankind.

19

The Jaws of Hell

The next night Jesus and I walked into the jaws of hell.

Jesus said, "We are almost through hell, my child. I will not show you all of hell. But what I have shown you, I want you to tell the world. Tell them hell is real. Tell them this report is real."

As we walked, we stopped on a hill overlooking a small valley. As far as I could see there were piles of human souls lining the sides of this hill. I could hear their cries. Loud noises filled the place. Jesus said, "My child, this is the jaws of hell. Every time the mouth of hell is opened, you will hear that loud noise."

The souls were trying to get out but could not, for they were embedded in the sides of hell.

173

As Jesus spoke, I saw many dark forms falling down past us and landing with a thud at the bottom of the hill. Demons with great chains were dragging souls away. Jesus said, "Those are the souls that have just died on earth and are arriving in hell. This activity goes on day and night."

Suddenly, a great silence filled the place. Jesus said, "I love you, My child, and I want you to tell the people of earth about hell."

I looked far down into the jaws of hell through a kind of porthole in the sides of the jaws. Cries of pain and torment came up from there. When will this end? I wondered. I would be so glad to rest from it all.

Then, all at once, I felt very lost. I cannot say how I knew, but I knew with all my heart that Jesus was gone. I felt very sad. I turned to where He had been. Sure enough, there was no Jesus! "Oh no!" I cried, "Not again! O Jesus, where are You?"

What you are about to read will frighten you. I pray it will frighten you enough to make you a believer. I pray you will repent of your sins so you will not go to that awful place. I pray you will believe me, for I do not want this to happen to anyone else. I love you and hope you will awake before it is too late.

If you are a Christian and you are reading this, be sure of your salvation. Be ready to meet the Lord at all times, for sometimes there is no time to repent. Keep your light burning and your lamp full of oil. Be ready, for you do not know when He will return. If you are not born again, read John 3:16-19, and call upon the Lord. He will save you from this place of torment.

As I cried out to Jesus, I began to run down the hill looking for Him. I was stopped by a large demon with a chain. He laughed and said, "You have nowhere to run, woman. Jesus is not here to save you. You are in hell forever."

"Oh no," I cried, "let me go!" I fought him with all my strength but was soon bound with a chain and thrown to the ground. As I lay there, a strange, gooey film began to cover my body with a stink so horrible I felt sick. I did not know what was going to happen.

And then I felt my flesh and skin begin to fall off my bones! I screamed and screamed in abject horror. "O Jesus," I called out, "where are You?"

I looked at myself and saw that holes were beginning to appear all over my remaining flesh. I began to turn a dirty-gray color, and gray flesh fell off me. There were holes in my sides, my legs, my hands and my arms. I cried out, "Oh, no! I am in hell forever! Oh, no!"

I began to feel the worms inside me and looked to find that my bones were teeming with them. Even when I could not see them, I knew they were there. I tried to pull them off me, but more came to fill the place. I could actually feel the decay in my body.

Yes, I knew everything and could remember exactly what had happened on earth. I could feel, see, smell, hear and taste the torments of hell. I could see inside myself. I was only a dirty skeletal form, yet I could feel all that was happening to me. I saw others like myself. There were souls as far as I could see.

I cried out in great pain, "O Jesus! Please help me, Jesus." I wanted to die, but I could not. I felt the fire kindle again in my legs. I screamed, "Where are You, Jesus?" I rolled about on the ground and cried along with all the others. We lay in the jaws of hell in little heaps, like thrown-away garbage. Unbearable pain gripped our souls.

I kept on screaming over and over again, "Where are You, Jesus? Where are You, Jesus?"

I wondered if this was just a dream? Would I wake up? Was I really in hell? Had I committed some great sin against God and lost my salvation? What had happened? Did I sin against the Holy Ghost? I remembered all the Bible teaching I had ever heard. I knew my family was somewhere above me. In horror I realized I was in hell just like all the other souls I had seen and spoken to.

It felt so strange to be able to see completely through my body. The worms had begun to crawl on me again. I could feel them crawling. I screamed with fear and pain.

Just then a demon said, "Your Jesus let you down, didn't He? Well, you are Satan's property now!" Evil laughter came from him as he picked up my form and placed me on top of something.

I soon found out that I was on the back of the living-dead form of some kind of animal. The animal, like me, was dingy gray, full of filth and decaying, dead flesh. A horrible odor filled the dirty air. The animal took me high up on a ledge. I thought, O Lord, where are You?

We passed many souls crying out to be saved. I heard the loud sound of hell's jaws opening and more souls fell past me. My hands were tied behind my back.

The pain was not constant—it came suddenly and went away suddenly. I screamed each time the pains came and waited with dread when they subsided.

I thought, How will I get out? What is ahead? Is this the end? What have I done to deserve hell? "O Lord, where are You?" I cried in pain.

I cried, but no tears came—only dry sobs shook my body. The animal stopped in front of something. I looked up to see a beautiful room full of extravagant riches and shining jewels. In the center of this room was a beautiful woman dressed in queen's apparel. I wondered in my state of despair what this was.

I said, "Woman, please help me." She came close and spit in my form of a face. She cursed me and said foul things to me. "O Lord, what is next?" I cried. An evil laugh came from her.

Right before my eyes the woman changed into a man, a cat, a horse, a snake, a rat and a young man. Whatever she chose to be, she was. She had great evil power. At the top of her room was written "Queen of Satan."

The animal moved on for what seemed like hours, and then it stopped. With a jolt, I was thrown off the animal and onto the ground. I looked up and saw an army of men on horseback riding toward me. I was forced to the side as they passed. They also were skeletons with the dingy-gray color of death.

After they passed, I was picked up from the ground and put in a cell. As someone locked the door, I looked around the cell in horror and cried. I prayed, but without hope. I cried and repented a thousand times for my sins. Yes, I thought of many things I could have done to lead others to Christ and to help someone when they needed me. I repented of the things I had done and the things I had left undone.

"O Lord, save me," I cried. Over and over I called out to God to help me. I could not see Him or feel Him. I was in hell just like the rest of the ones I had seen. I fell to the floor in pain and cried. I felt I was forever lost.

Hours went by, and every so often the loud sound came again, and other souls fell into hell. I kept calling out, "Jesus, where are You?" No answer came. The worms began again to crawl inside my spirit form. I could feel them all inside me.

Death was everywhere. I had no flesh, no organs, no blood, no body and no hope. I kept pulling worms out of my skeleton form. I knew everything that was happening, and I wanted to die but could not. My soul would be alive forever.

I began to sing about the life and the power in the blood of Jesus, which is able to save from sin. When I did, large demons with spears came and screamed, "Stop it!" They stabbed me with the spears, and I felt hot flashes of fire as the points went into my form. Over and over they stabbed me.

They chanted, "Satan is god here. We hate Jesus and all He stands for!"

When I would not stop singing, they took me out of the cell and dragged me to a large opening. "If you do not be quiet," they said, "your torments will be greater."

I stopped singing, and at long last they put me back into the cell. I remembered a Bible verse about fallen angels who were reserved in chains until final judgment. I wondered if this was my judgment. "Lord, save the people on earth," I cried. "Wake them up before it is too late." Many Scriptures came to my mind, but I feared the demons and did not say them.

Moans and screams filled the dirty air. A rat crawled near me. I kicked it away. I thought of my husband and children. "O God, don't let them come here," I cried, for I knew for sure I was in hell.

God could not hear me. The ears of the Almighty are closed to the cries of hell, I thought. If only someone would listen.

A large rat ran up my leg and bit me. I screamed and pulled it off. There was a great flash of pain.

A fire out of nowhere began to slowly burn toward me. Seconds, minutes, hours went by. I was a sinner, gone to hell. "O death, please come," I cried. My cries seemed to fill the whole jaws of hell. Others joined in my cries—lost forever—no way! I wanted to die, but I could not.

I fell to the floor in a heap, feeling all these torments. I heard the jaws open again, and more souls came in. The fires burned me now, and a new pain came. I knew all that was happening. I had a sharp, sound mind. I knew all these things, and I knew that when souls die on earth and are not saved from their sins, they come here.

"O my God, save me," I cried. "Please save all of us."

I remembered my whole life and all those who had told me about Jesus. I remembered praying for the sick and how Jesus had healed them. I remembered His words of love and comfort and His faithfulness.

If only I were, or had been, more like Jesus, I would not be here, I thought. I thought of all the good things God had given me—how He gave me the very air I breathed, food, children, a home, and good things to enjoy. But, if He is a good God, then why am I here? I had no strength to get up, but my soul kept crying, "Let me out of here."

I knew that life was going on above me and somewhere my friends and family were going about their normal lives. I knew there was laughter, love and kindness somewhere up there. But even that began to fade away in the awful pain.

Semi-darkness and a dim, dirty fog filled this part of hell. A dim yellow light was everywhere, and a smell of rotting flesh and corruption was almost too much to bear. Minutes seemed like hours, and hours stretched into an eternity. O when would this stop?

I had no sleep, no rest, no food and no water. I had a great hunger and was thirstier than I could ever remember being in all my life. I was so tired and so sleepy—but the pain went on and on. Each time the jaws opened they dumped another load of lost humanity into hell, I wondered if anyone I knew was among them. Would they bring my husband here?

Hours had gone by since I arrived in the jaws of hell. But then I noticed that a light was beginning to fill the room. All at once the fire stopped, the rat ran away, and the pain left my body. I looked for any avenue of escape, but there was none.

I wondered what was happening. I looked out the portholes of hell, knowing this was something dreadful. And then hell began to shake, and the burning fire came again. Again, the snakes and rats and worms! Unbearable pain filled my soul as the torments started again.

"O God, let me die," I cried as I began to bang the earthen floor of my cell with my bony hands. I screamed and cried, but no one knew or cared.

All at once I was lifted from the cell by an unseen force. When I regained consciousness, the Lord and I were standing beside my house. I cried out, "Why, Lord, why?" and fell at His feet in despair.

Jesus said, "Peace, be still." At once I was at peace. He lifted me tenderly, and I fell asleep in His arms.

When I awoke the next day, I was very sick. For days I relived the horrors of hell and its torment. At night I would wake up screaming and saying there were worms crawling in me. I was so afraid of hell.

20

Heaven

I was sick for many days after I was left in the jaws of hell. I had to have the lights left on when I slept. I needed the Bible with me at all times, and I read it constantly. My soul was in severe shock. I knew now what the lost endured when they went to hell to stay.

Jesus would say, "Peace, be still," and peace would flood my soul. But a few minutes later I would wake up screaming, hysterical with fear.

During this time, I knew I was never alone—Jesus was always there. But even with that knowledge, I sometimes could not feel His presence. And I was so afraid of having to go back to hell that I was fearful to even have Jesus near me sometimes.

I tried to tell others about my experiences in hell. They would not listen to me. I begged them, "Please, repent of your sins before it's too late." It was difficult for anyone to believe what I told them of the torment that I had been through and how Jesus had told me to write about hell.

The Lord assured me that He was the Lord who healed me. And though I believed I would never fully recover, healing did come.

And then it happened again. Again I was in the spirit with the Lord Jesus, and we were soaring high up in the sky.

Jesus said, "I want to show you the love and goodness of God and parts of heaven. I want you to see the wondrous works of the Lord, which are so beautiful to behold."

Ahead of us I saw two giant planets, beautiful and glorious in all their splendor. God himself was the light there.

An angel met us and said to me, "See the goodness and kindness of the Lord your God. His mercy endures forever." There was such a strong sense of love and tenderness about the angel that I was about to weep when he spoke again, "Behold the power and might and majesty of God. Let me show you the place He has created for the children."

All at once there was a large planet looming before us, a planet as large as the earth. And then I heard the voice of the Father saying, "The Father, the Son and the Holy Ghost are all one. The Father and the Son are one, and the Father and the Holy Ghost are one. I sent My Son to die on a cross so that no one needed to be lost.

"But," He said with a smile, "I was about to show you the place I made for My children. I care greatly about all children. I care when a mother loses a child, even as the fruit of your womb, My child, was cast before its time. You see, I know all things, and I care.

"From the time there is life in the womb, I know. I know about the babies that are murdered while they are still in their mother's bodies—the aborted lives that are cast off and unwanted. I know about the stillborn and those children who are born with crippling defects. From the time of conception, that is a soul.

"My angels go down and bring the children to Me when they die. I have a place where they can grow, learn and be loved. I give them whole bodies and restore whatever parts they are missing. I give them glorified bodies."

All over the planet there was a feeling of being loved, a sense of perfect well-being. Everything was perfect. Here and there amid the lush green grass and the pools of crystal clear water were playgrounds with marble seats and highly polished wooden benches to sit on.

And there were children. Everywhere one looked, there were children going about all kinds of activities. Each child wore a spotless white robe and sandals. The white robes were so bright they glistened in the magnificent light on the planet. A profusion of color everywhere accented the whiteness of the children's robes. Angels were the keepers of the gates, and the children's names were all written in a book.

I saw children learning the Word of God and being taught music from a golden book. I was surprised to see animals of all sorts coming up to the children or sitting beside them while they were in this angelic school.

There were no tears and no sorrow. Everything was supremely beautiful, and joy and happiness were everywhere.

Then the angel showed me another planet which glowed like a great light before me. The light shone with the radiance of a million stars, and everything on the planet was beautiful and alive.

In the distance I saw two mountains made of pure gold, while closer to me were two golden gates embedded with diamonds and other precious stones. I knew that this was the new earth and that the city which lay in splendor before me was the New Jerusalem—the city of God come down to earth.

And then I was back on the old earth—earth as it was before the final fires that would purge it and purify it for God's glorious purpose. And here too was a new Jerusalem, the capital city of the millennium. And I saw people coming out of caves and from the mountains and making their way toward this city.

Here Jesus was King, and all the nations of the earth brought Him gifts and paid Him homage.

Jesus gave me the interpretation of my vision. He said, "Soon I will return and take back with Me to heaven first the righteous dead, then after them those that are alive and remain will be caught up to be with Me in the air. Following that, the Antichrist will reign upon the earth for an appointed time, and there will be tribulations such as have never been before, nor will ever be again.

"And then I will return with My saints, and Satan will be cast into the bottomless pit, where he will remain for a thousand years. During that thousand years I will reign over the earth from Jerusalem. When the millennium is past, Satan will be released for a season, and I will defeat him by the brightness of My coming. The old earth will pass away.

"Behold, there shall be a new earth and a New Jerusalem coming down upon it—and I will reign forever and ever."

21

False Religion

The Lord said, "If the people of the earth will listen to Me and repent of their sins, I will hold back the workings of the Antichrist and the beast till there comes a time of refreshing. Didn't the people of Ninevah repent at the preaching of Jonah? I am the same yesterday, today and forever. Repent, and I will send a time of blessing."

Then I heard Jesus say, "My people should love one another and help one another. They must hate sin and love the sinner. By this love shall all men know that you are My disciples."

As Jesus spoke, the earth opened, and we were back in hell. I saw a hillside filled with dead tree trunks, and all around it was gray dirt. I saw also small pits in the side of the hill, and the gray forms of people walking and talking.

I followed Jesus on a very crooked and dirty trail that led up the side of the gray hill. As we drew nearer, I saw that the people were whole, but dead. They were composed of gray, dead flesh, and they were bound together with a rope of bondage, a kind of cord of gray matter that wound around and around and all about the people on the hill. While there was no fire in sight, I knew that this was a part of hell, for dead flesh fell from the bones of the people there and then grew back really fast. Death was everywhere, but the people did not seem to notice—they were deeply engrossed in conversation.

Jesus said, "Let's listen to what they're saying."

One man said to another, "Did you hear about this man Jesus who came to take away sin?"

Another responded, "I know Jesus. He washed my sins away. In fact, I don't know what I'm doing here."

"Nor do I," said the first man.

Another said, "I tried to witness to my neighbor about Jesus, but he wouldn't even listen. When his wife died, he came to me to borrow the money for her funeral, but I remembered that Jesus had said we should be wise as serpents and harmless as doves. So I turned him away. I knew he would spend the money for something else anyway. We have to be good stewards of our money, you know."

The first man who had spoken now spoke again. "Yes, brother," he said, "a boy at our church needed clothes and shoes, but his father drinks, so I refused to buy anything for his son—we really taught that man a lesson."

"Well," said another man, as he held the rope of bondage in his hands and twisted it all about him nervously, "we must always teach others to live like Jesus. That man had no right to drink. Let him suffer."

Jesus said, "O foolish people and slow of heart, awaken to the truth, and love one another with fervent love. Help the helpless. Give to those in need without any thought of getting anything in return.

"If you will repent, O earth, I will bless you and not curse you. Awaken from your sleep, and come unto Me. Humble yourselves and bow your hearts before Me, and I will come and live with you. You will be My people, and I will be your God."

22

The Mark of the Beast

I heard the Lord say, "My Spirit will not always strive with man. Come and see the beast.

"During the last days an evil beast will arise out of the earth and deceive many from every nation upon the earth. He will demand that everyone receive his mark, the number *666*, placed in their hands or on their foreheads. Anyone who takes the mark will belong to the beast and will be thrown with him into the lake of fire which burns with fire and brimstone.

"The beast will arise to the acclamation of the world, for he will bring peace and prosperity such as none can remember. When he has gained world dominion, those without his mark in their foreheads or their hands will not be able to buy food, clothes, cars, houses or anything else that is bought. Neither will they be able to sell anything they own to anyone else unless they have the mark.

"The Lord God expressly declares that those who take the mark have affirmed their allegiance to the beast and will be cut off from the Lord God forever. They will have their place with the unbelievers and workers of iniquity. The mark states simply that those who possess it have rejected God and have turned to the beast for sustenance.

"The beast and his followers will persecute those who refuse the mark and will kill many of them. Whatever pressures they can bring to bear will be used to force believers of the true God to be marked. Children and infants will be killed before the eyes of the parents who refuse to take the mark. There will be a time of great mourning.

"Those who possess the mark will be forced to turn over their possessions to the beast in exchange for a promise that the beast will meet all the needs of his followers.

"Some of you will weaken and surrender to the beast and receive his mark in your hand or forehead. You will say, 'God will forgive. God will understand.' But I will not repent of My Word. I have warned you repeatedly through the mouths of My prophets and ministers of the gospel. Repent now while it is still day, for the night comes when judgment will be set forever.

"If you do not obey the beast and refuse to take his mark, I will take care of you. I do not say that many will not have to die for their faith in these times, for many will be beheaded for trusting the Lord God. But blessed are those who die in the Lord, for great will be their reward.

"True, there will be a time of peace and prosperity during which the beast will gain popularity and esteem. He will make the problems of the world as though they were naught—but the peace will end in bloodshed and the prosperity in great famine across the land.

"Fear not what man can do to you, but fear him who can cast your soul and body into hell. For though there is great persecution and though tribulations are multiplied, I will deliver you through them all.

"But before that evil day, I will raise up a mighty army that will worship Me in spirit and in truth. The army of the Lord will do great exploits and wonderful things for Me. Therefore, come together and worship Me in spirit and in truth. Bring in the fruits of righteousness, and give Me what is rightfully Mine, and I will keep you from the evil hour. Repent now and be saved from the terrible things which will befall the rebellious and the unsaved.

"The wages of sin is death, but the gift of God is eternal life. Call on Me while you may, and I will accept you and forgive you. I love you and do not desire that you should be lost.

"Believe this report and live. Choose you this day whom you will serve."

23

The Return of Christ

I saw the coming of the Lord. I heard His call like
the sound of a trumpet and the voice of an arch-
angel. And the whole earth shook, and out of the
graves came the righteous dead to meet their Lord
in the air. For hours it seemed, I heard the horns
blow, and the earth and the sea gave up their dead.
The Lord Jesus Christ stood atop the clouds in
vestments of fire and beheld the glorious scene.

I heard the sound of trumpets again. As I
watched, those who were alive and remained on the
earth ascended to meet them. I saw the redeemed as
millions of points of light converging on a gathering
place in the sky. There the angels gave them robes
of purest white. There was great rejoicing.

It was given to the angels to keep order, and
they seemed to be everywhere and giving special

attention to the risen ones. A new body was given to the redeemed, and they were transformed as they passed through the air.

Great joy and happiness filled the heavens, and the angels sang, "Glory to the King of Kings!"

High in the heavens I beheld a large spiritual body—it was the body of Christ. And the body was lying on its back on a bed, and blood dripped to the earth. I knew that this was the slain body of our Lord. And then the body grew larger and larger until it filled the heavens. And going into and out of it were the millions of the redeemed.

I watched in astonishment as millions climbed up stairs to the body and filled it, beginning with the feet and continuing through the legs, the arms, the stomach, the heart and the head. And when it was full, I saw that it was filled with men and women from every nation, people and tongue on the earth. And with a mighty voice they praised the Lord.

Millions were seated before a throne, and I saw angels as they brought the books from which judgment was read. There was the mercy seat, and rewards were given to many.

Then as I watched, darkness covered the face of the earth, and demon forces were everywhere. Countless evil spirits had been loosed from their prison and spilled forth onto the earth. I heard the Lord say, "Woe to the inhabitants of the earth, for Satan has come to dwell among you."

I saw an angry beast, and he poured out his venom upon all the earth. Hell shook in its fury, and from a bottomless pit came swarming hordes of evil creatures to blacken the earth with their vast numbers. Men and women ran crying into the hills, the caves and the mountains. And there were wars upon the earth, and famine and death.

At last I saw horses of fire and chariots in the heavens. The earth trembled, and the sun turned red like blood. And an angel said, "Hear, O earth, the King is coming!"

And there appeared in the sky the King of Kings and Lord of Lords, and with Him were the saints of all ages, clad in purest white. And I remembered that every eye shall behold Him and every knee shall bow before Him.

Then the angels put in their sickles and harvested the ripened grain—which is the end of the world.

Jesus said, "Repent and be saved, for the kingdom of God is at hand. My will and My Word will be performed. Prepare the way of the Lord."

And I thought, We must love one another. We must be firm in the truth and correct our children in the light of the soon coming of Christ. For surely the King is coming!

24

God's Final Plea

Jesus said, "Charge them that are in the world that they be not haughty nor trust in uncertain riches but to put their trust in the living God, who gives us richly all things to enjoy. Walk in the Spirit, and you will not fulfill the lust of the flesh.

"Be not deceived; God is not mocked. For whatever a man sows that will he also reap. Sow to the flesh, and you will reap corruption. Sow to the Spirit, and you will reap life everlasting. The works of the flesh are adultery, fornication, uncleanness idolatry, witchcraft, wrath, envying, drunkenness, reveling and such like. Those who do these things will not inherit the kingdom of God.

"The fruit of the Spirit are these: love, joy, peace, patience, gentleness, goodness, faithfulness, meekness and self-control. They that are Christ's have crucified the flesh with its lusts.

"When the Word of God is fulfilled, then the end will come. No man knows the day nor the hour when the Son of God will return to the earth. Not even the Son knows, for that is known only by the Father. The Word is quickly being fulfilled. Come as a little child, and let Me cleanse you from the works of the flesh. Say to Me, 'Lord Jesus, come into my heart and forgive me of my sins. I know that I am a sinner, and I repent of my sins. Wash me in Your blood, and make me clean. I have sinned against heaven and before You and am not worthy to be called a son. I receive You by faith as my Savior.'

"I will give you pastors after My own heart, and I will be your Shepherd. You will be My people, and I will be your God. Read the Word, and forsake not the assembling of yourselves. Give your whole life to Me, and I will keep you. I will never leave or forsake you."

People, by one Spirit, we have access to the Father. I pray that all of you will come and give your hearts to the Lord.

25

Visions of Heaven

Some of the following visions were given to me before Jesus took me into hell. Some of them came near the end of my journey through hell.

Similarity to God

I received this heavenly vision while in deep prayer, meditation and worship.

The glory of the Lord descended upon the place where I was praying. Great billows of fire, bright lights and majestic power came before my eyes. In the center of the fire and the lights was the throne of God. On the throne was a similarity of God. Joy, peace and love flowed from God Almighty.

The air around the throne was filled with baby cherubim, singing and kissing the Lord upon His face, His hands and His feet. The song they sang was "Holy, holy, holy is the Lord God Almighty." The cherubim had tongues of fire sitting on their heads and on the tips of each tiny wing. The motion of their wings seemed synchronized with the movement of the power and glory of the Lord.

A cherub flew to me and touched my eyes.

Golden Mountains

In a vision I looked far out over the earth. I could see that for many miles the land was thirsty for rain. The ground was cracked, dry and barren. There were no trees or vegetation of any kind to be seen.

Then I was allowed to see beyond the dry land, all the way to heaven. There, side by side and touching at their bases, were two giant mountains. I do not know their height, but they were very, very high. I drew closer to the mountains and discovered that they were made of solid gold—gold so pure it was transparent.

Through and beyond the mountains I saw a brilliant white light, and the light expanded to fill the universe. I felt in my heart that this was the base upon which heaven sits.

Men fight over a small gold ring, but God owns all the gold.

The Building of a Mansion

While at prayer I received this vision. I saw angels reading the record of the works we do here on earth. Some of the angels had wings, while some did not. Some were big, and some were little, but all their faces were different. Like the people here on earth, the angels could be identified by their facial features.

I saw the angels busily cutting extremely large diamonds and placing them in the foundations of beautiful mansions. The diamonds were a foot thick and two feet long and very beautiful. Each time a soul is won for God, a diamond is added to the soulwinner's mansion. No labor is in vain when it is done for God.

Gates of Heaven

At another time when I was in prayer, I saw this heavenly vision. I was in the spirit and an angel came to me and took me into the heavens. Again there were magnificent scenes of billowing light and dazzling glory such as I had seen behind the solid-gold mountains. It was awe-inspiring to behold the power of God displayed.

As the angel and I approached two giant gates in a huge wall, we saw two exceptionally large angels with swords. They were about fifty feet tall, and their hair was spun gold. The gates were so high I could not see the tops of them. They were the most beautiful works of art I have ever seen. They were hand-carved, with intricate folds, drapes, layers and carvings, and were studded with pearls, diamonds, rubies, sapphires and other gems. Everything on the gates was in perfect balance, and the gates opened outward. An angel with a book in his hand came out from behind the gates. After checking the book, the angel nodded, confirming that I could enter.

Reader, you cannot get into heaven if your name is not in the Lamb's Book of Life.

The File Room

In a vision, an angel took me to heaven and showed me a very large room with walls of solid gold. Alphabetical letters were engraved here and there on the walls. The scene was much like a huge library, but the books were embedded into the wall instead of being shelved.

Angels in long robes were taking books out of the walls and studying them closely. There seemed to be a rigid order in what they did. I noticed that the books had thick gold covers and some of the pages were red. The books were very beautiful.

The angel with me said these books were a record of the lives of every person who has ever been born on earth. I was told there were more rooms elsewhere with even more records. From time to time the archangels brought the records before God for His approval or disapproval. The books contained prayer requests, prophecies, attitudes, growth in the Lord, souls led to Christ, the fruit of the Spirit and much more. Everything we do on earth is recorded in one of the books by the angels.

Every so often an angel would take a book down and wash the pages with a soft cloth. The washed pages turned red.

A Heavenly Ladder

The Spirit of the Lord brought me the following vision. I saw a large spiritual ladder which descended from heaven to earth. On one side of the ladder angels were coming down to the earth, while on the other side they were going up.

The angels on the ladder had no wings, but every angel had a book with a name written on the front cover. Some of the angels seemed to be giving directions and answering questions posed to them by the other angels. Once the directions were received and their questions answered, they disappeared.

I also saw other ladders in other parts of the earth. Angels were in constant motion, ascending and descending. The angels moved with boldness and authority, since they were messengers with orders from God.

26

A Prophecy from Jesus

When Jesus first appeared to me, He said, "Kathryn, you have been chosen by the Father to accompany me through the depths of hell. I will show you many things which I desire the world to know about hell and about heaven. I will tell you what to write so that this book will be a true record of what these unknown places are really like. My Spirit will reveal secrets about eternity, judgment, love, death and life hereafter."

The message of the Lord to a lost world is this: "I do not desire that you go to hell. I made you for My own joy and for everlasting fellowship. You are My creation, and I love you. Call upon Me while I am near, and I will hear and answer you. I want to forgive you and bless you."

To those who are born again, the Lord says: "Forget not the assembling of yourselves. Come together and pray and study My Word. Worship Me in the spirit of holiness."

The Lord says to the churches and the nations: "My angels fight always for the heirs of salvation and for those who will become heirs. I do not change. I am the same yesterday, today and forever. Seek Me, and I will pour out My Spirit upon you. Your sons and your daughters will prophesy. I will do great things among you."

If you are unsaved, please take the time right now to kneel before the Lord and ask Him to forgive you of your sins and make you His child. Whatever the cost, you should determine now to make heaven your eternal home. Hell is awful, and hell is real.

Closing Words

I wish to assure you again that the things you have read in this book are true. Hell is a real place of burning torment. But I would also like to tell you that heaven is equally real and can be your home for eternity.

As God's handmaiden, I have yielded myself to the leading of the Lord Jesus Christ and have faithfully recorded those things which He has shown me and told me.

For best results you should read this book along with your Bible and balance what is written here with the Holy Scriptures. May God use this book for His glory.

Mary Kathryn Baxter

Rev. 20:13-15   Proverbs 7:27   Matthew 23:33
Matthew 10:28   Proverbs 9:18   Mark 9:43-48
Luke 12:5   Isaiah 5:14   Romans 10:9-10
Luke 16:20-31   Isaiah 14:12-15   1 John 1:9
Psalm 9:17   Matthew 5:22

About the Author

Mary Kathryn Baxter was born in Chattanooga, Tennessee. She was brought up in the house of God. While she was still young, her mother taught her about Jesus Christ and His salvation.

Kathryn was born again at the age of nineteen. After serving the Lord for several years, she backslid for a season. The Spirit of the Lord would not release her, and she came back and gave her life anew to Christ. She still serves Him faithfully.

In the mid-1960s Kathryn moved with her family to Detroit, Michigan, where she lived for a time. She later moved to Belleville, Michigan, where she began to have visions from God.

In 1976, while she was living in Belleville, Jesus appeared to her in human form, in dreams, in visions, and in revelations. Since that time, she has received many visitations from the Lord. During those visits He has shown her the depths, degrees, levels, and torments of lost souls in hell. She has also received many visions of heaven, the Great Tribulation, and the end of time.

During one period of her life, Jesus appeared to her each night for for y nights. He revealed to her the horrors of hell and the glories of heaven. He told her that this message is for the whole world.

Ministers, leaders, and saints of the Lord speak very highly of her and her ministry. The movement of the Holy Spirit is emphasized in all her services, and many miracles have occurred in them. The gifts of the Holy Spirit with demonstrations of power are manifested in her meetings as the Spirit of God leads and empowers her. She loves the Lord with all her heart, mind, soul, and strength and desires above all else to be a soulwinner for Jesus Christ.

She is truly a dedicated handmaiden of the Lord. Her calling is specifically in the area of dreams, visions, and revelations. She was ordained as a minister in 1983 at the Full Gospel Church of God in Taylor, Michigan. She now ministers with the National Church of God in Washington, D.C.

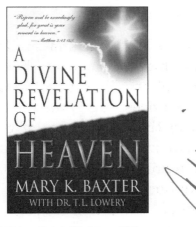

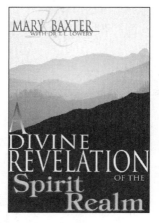

OTHER POWERFUL BOOKS

from Whitaker House

Una Revelación Divina del Infierno
by Mary K. Baxter
ISBN: 0-88368-288-5
Trade
144 pages

Una Revelación Divina del Cielo
by Mary K. Baxter
ISBN: 0-88368-572-8
Trade
208 pages

Una Revelación Divina del Reino Espiritual
by Mary K. Baxter
ISBN: 0-88368-672-4
Trade
208 pages

ANOTHER POWERFUL *B*OOK
from Whitaker House

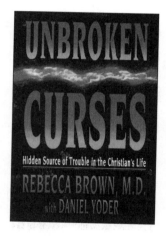

Unbroken Curses
Dr. Rebecca Brown

Countless Christians are plagued by a variety of unexplained adverse circumstances. Usually they are unaware that their plight is the result of an unbroken curse that has been placed upon them and perhaps upon their families. This book shows you the necessary biblical steps to identify, prevent, and break every type of curse.

ISBN: 0-88368-372-5 • Trade • 176 pages

TROUBLE at TABLE 5

#2:
Busted by Breakfast

Check out all the
TROUBLE at TABLE 5
books!

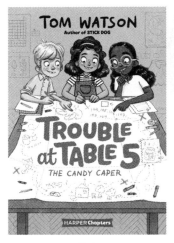

#1

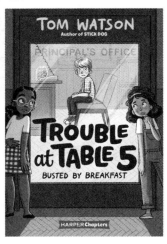

#2

Read more books by **Tom Watson**

#1–12

#1–5

TROUBLE at TABLE 5

#2:
Busted by Breakfast

by **Tom Watson**

illustrated by
Marta Kissi

An Imprint of HarperCollins*Publishers*

Dedicated to Elizabeth
(IASPOY)

Trouble at Table 5 #2: Busted by Breakfast
Text copyright © 2020 by Tom Watson
Illustrations copyright © 2020 by HarperCollins Publishers
Illustrations by Marta Kissi
www.harperchapters.com
Library of Congress Control Number: 2019950274
ISBN 978-0-06-295344-5 — ISBN 978-0-06-295343-8 (pbk.)
Typography by Torberg Davern
20 21 22 23 24   PC/LSCC   10 9 8 7 6 5 4

First Edition